Early in the Season

EDWARD HOAGLAND

INTRODUCTION BY STEPHEN HUME

Early in the Season

A BRITISH COLUMBIA JOURNAL

Douglas & McIntyre

VANCOUVER/TORONTO/BERKELEY

For A.F., who chanced the Yellowhead Route with me in 1960.

Copyright © 2008 by Edward Hoagland
Introduction copyright © 2008 by Stephen Hume

08 09 10 11 12   5 4 3 2 1

Douglas & McIntyre Ltd.
2323 Quebec Street, Suite 201
Vancouver, British Columbia
Canada v5T 4S7
www.douglas-mcintyre.com

Library and Archives Canada Cataloguing in Publication
Hoagland, Edward
Early in the season: a British Columbia journal/Edward Hoagland;
introduction by Stephen Hume.

ISBN 978-1-55365-428-5

1. British Columbia, Northern—Description and travel. 2. Hoagland, Edward—
Travel—British Columbia, Northern. 3. Pioneers—British Columbia,
Northern—History. 4. Frontier and pioneer life—British Columbia, Northern.
5. British Columbia, Northern—Social life and customs. I. Title.
FC3817.4.H59 2008   917.1104'4   C2008-903325-6

Copy editing by Derek Fairbridge
Jacket and text design by Naomi MacDougall
Main jacket illustration by Walter-Joseph Phillips from *Colour in the Canadian Rockies* by
Walter J. Phillips and Frederick Niven (Toronto: Thomas Nelson and Sons [Canada] Ltd., 1937);
inset photograph courtesy of Glenbow Archives NA-4868-183
Printed and bound in Canada by Friesens
Printed on acid-free paper that is forest friendly (100% post-consumer recycled paper)
and has been processed chlorine free
Distributed in the U.S. by Publishers Group West

A portion of this book first appeared under the title "Miles from Nowhere"
in *The American Scholar*, Summer 2006.

We gratefully acknowledge the financial support of the Canada Council for the Arts, the British Columbia Arts Council, the Province of British Columbia through the Book Publishing Tax Credit, and the Government of Canada through the Book Publishing Industry Development Program (BPIDP) for our publishing activities.

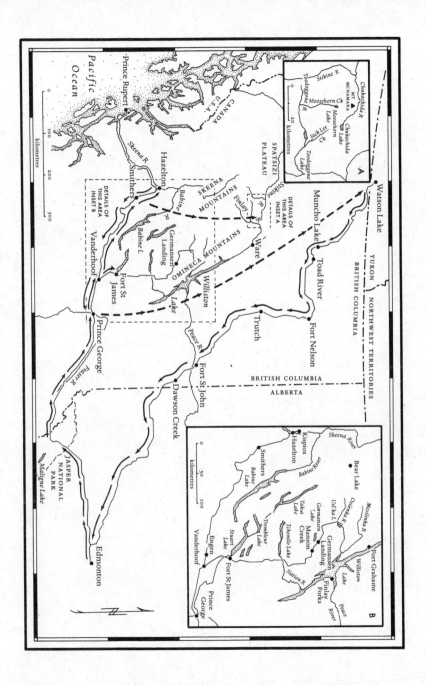

Introduction

BY STEPHEN HUME

THE CRUMPLED landscape that is Edward Hoagland's British Columbia sprawls in splendid chaos across an area that if magically transported to, say, Western Europe, would just about cover France, Germany, and the Low Countries combined. Its boreal forest alone is the size of Germany. The snowmelt from seven major mountain ranges and their glaciers, augmented by the runoff from immense watersheds, seethes through convoluted bedrock, carving its way toward both Arctic and Pacific oceans and along the way braiding itself into some of the biggest and most powerful rivers on the North American continent. Submerge your head briefly in any of those icy torrents and you can hear the hiss and whisper of hard glacial silt abrading the world, still teasing out the gold with which the rivers seed their bars.

Fourteen definable biogeoclimatic zones change vertically as well as by longitude and latitude, from alpine tundra to temperate coastal rain forest and from subarctic black spruce to antelope-brush deserts. The province is the most biologically diverse in Canada, home to tens of thousands of species. Many are uniquely adapted to a plethora of microclimates; some are found nowhere else on Earth.

Of this territory, more than half a million square kilometres—an area larger than France—are officially designated the province's North. In its time, the region has been called by many names. It is Denendeh, "our land," in the Athapaskan group of languages spoken by the Dene, "the people," whose hunting ancestors have left their footprints on it since the beginning of what we construe as time. Fur traders who first arrived in the eighteenth century called it New Caledonia because of its resemblance, they thought, to a Scotland they had never seen. Prospectors stampeding north from California through the Cariboo in the nineteenth century, lured by the rich deposits of placer gold, the flour, flake, and nuggets washing down the rivers, called it The Stickeen. The country teems with an astonishing variety of wildlife—lynx, grizzlies, mountain caribou, huge sturgeon, timber wolves, moose, black bears, elk, mountain goats, fishers and pine martens, sockeye and spring salmon that struggle a thousand kilometres against the current to spawn, Stone sheep, bison, ravens, ospreys, eagles, and wolverines. Small surprise that wildlife biologists, naturalists, outfitters, hunters, and ecologists, all equally mesmerized by the abundance and diversity, call what survives as the continent's last intact large-scale ecosystem "the Serengeti of the North."

Whatever the preferred name, the region sweeps westward from the Peace River, where the aspen grove prairies of the Great Plains break against the Rocky Mountains, to the glittering icefields of the St. Elias range. These westernmost mountains, the roof of the continent, represent the first known European sighting of the province's northern mainland, recorded by Vitus Bering on his doomed expedition from Siberia in 1741. Southward, the region extends from the rugged and remote Franklin Mountains of the Yukon and Northwest Territories, spilling in high drama across a spectacular jumble of snow-clad ranges, plateaus, trenches, lava flows, and Ice Age rubble. Its southern boundary is a line that runs from the Yellowhead Pass through the Rockies to Prince Rupert on the Pacific, roughly following the upper Fraser, Nechako, and Skeena rivers.

Only four main roads and a couple of railways skirt this northern country. The Yellowhead Highway extends from Jasper, Alberta, through Prince George to Prince Rupert; the John Hart Highway links Prince George to Dawson Creek in Peace River country and the Great Plains; the Alaska Highway runs from Dawson Creek to Watson

Lake in the Yukon; and the Cassiar Highway runs from near New Hazelton to Upper Liard at the Yukon border. Within the quadrangle made by these principal roads, the map remains largely blank with respect to human habitation. A few mining camps, forestry outposts, native Indian settlements, and the decaying remains of long-ebbed gold rushes are the only evidence of a population that remains among the sparsest in Canada.

About 170,000 people, one sixth the population of tiny Rhode Island, live in B.C.'s North, whose area is 240 times larger than that smallest state in the American union. Most of B.C.'s northerners dwell in isolated communities strung along the roads that form the outer boundaries of the great quadrangle. Most of the four million people who occupy the rest of the province have never visited. Inside this area, except for the flooding behind hydro dams on the Peace and Nechako rivers, logging clear-cuts, a mill town, and mine sites, the country remains as wild as it was when Alexander Mackenzie first ventured through it on his dash to the Pacific Ocean in 1793. There are a few First Nations settlements, hunting camps, prospectors' claims, traplines, and a scattering of people who have either been there forever or came, as someone once observed, to play God or to hide from Him.

It was into this measureless solitude that Hoagland, a young American writer in search of raw materials for his next novel, travelled in 1966. He wasn't the first. Indeed, for a place that in its day was at the farthest edge of the known world, the North has a rich literary heritage.

Mackenzie's eloquent 1801 account of his journey up the Peace River, then the Parsnip, down the Fraser, then overland to Bella Coola in 1793, including a shrewd assessment of the country's future strategic value, almost certainly spurred President Thomas Jefferson to launch the Lewis and Clark Expedition west to the Columbia River mouth in 1804.

Simon Fraser, born in 1776 just a stone's throw from Bennington College in Vermont, where Hoagland would later teach writing, was instructed in 1805 to expand the North West Company's fur trade beyond the Rockies and to find a navigable route to the Pacific Ocean. The journal he kept from 1806 to 1808 reads like a Victorian boy's adventure novel. His expedition loses canoes in ice-choked rivers, suffers starvation and frostbite, and grizzly bears attack his voyageurs. Fraser is himself mistaken for a supernatural being, leads his men through perilous canyons that resemble the underworld, is confronted by painted warriors who seem to spring silently from the earth, quells mutiny, escapes ambushes, fends off attacking canoes with musket muzzles, and returns without having lost a man or killed an enemy.

His successor at what later became Fort St. James, Daniel Williams Harmon, was also born at Bennington. His journal of life in New Caledonia from 1810 to 1816 oscillates between tenderness and trauma. The epiphany in which he realizes he loves his Métis wife, Lisette Duval, and can never abandon her is as moving a testament to sentiment and the human heart as any. It runs counterpoint to grisly descriptions of tribal blood feuds and an inability to comprehend the stature of the powerful Carrier war chief and statesman, Kwah.

Samuel Black, infamous for violence in the fur trade wars, later shot dead at the age of sixty by a Shuswap Indian, wrote a colourful account of his exploration of the Finlay River in 1824. Robert Campbell, seduced to the frontier by a fur trade cousin's romantic tales, recounted boiling and eating the rawhide webbing from his snowshoes at Dease Lake in 1839. British adventurer R. Byron Johnson, who followed the first gold rush, provided a picaresque account of his rollicking trek north to the diggings and chastened trudge back in 1862. Father Adrian Gabriel Morice, an Oblate missionary at Fort St. James in 1880, learned the local aboriginal languages, devised a written form for Carrier, collected their oral histories and combined them with those of old-timers in the fur trade to create his lively and immensely readable *History of the Northern Interior of British Columbia*. Another Englishman, R.M. Patterson, wrote extensively of his travels through the remote North in the 1920s, and Lizette Hall collected and published the expressive stories of her Carrier people.

If Hoagland trekked to the North in search of wilderness experience, he soon found himself in one of the last places on Earth where it was still possible to survive by one's wits, hard work, luck, and the bounty of a stunningly beautiful but often unforgiving land. He was drawn, it turned out, less to the natural world he thought was his quest than to the fascinating array of characters he discovered inhabiting it. Remittance men and draft dodgers, expatriate Americans, the washed-up detritus of gold rushes, this-and-that trappers, hardscrabble storekeepers and gritty bush pilots, a direct descendent of Chief Kwah. They lived in outposts, encampments, and distant cabins out back of the outback. Many were relics of another time, the last survivors of a world that was vanishing even as they and their memories of it faded away. Hoagland describes them in a sweet essay of reminiscence for *Harper's Magazine* as "guys from the era of the First World War or the Depression, living on the Skeena River or the Stikine, in British Columbia and Alaska—the Spatsizi or the Omineca, the Klappan or the Kuskokwin, the Tanana or the Porcupine."

They were, he wrote, the kind of men who were inclined to wear their long johns all year long. They reeked of pungent woodsmoke, the poor man's mosquito repellant. And they were always "on the lookout for gold colorations in the creekbeds as we walked about, and before fall got well started they would be laying in a mammoth woodpile, and extra rations under the floorboards, and boiling and re-scenting their fur traps, then, after a hard frost, throwing caribou carcasses up on the pitched roof, where they'd keep." They were, in short, as distinctive and articulate in their sometimes loquacious, sometimes laconic ways as the pantheon of literary figures that had preceded him through the North. They told him stories, their own stories, stories about each other, about the bush, burnishing the whole dishevelled, unruly oral history of a unique place that they knew was on the downside of a descent into the grave along with its dwindling custodians.

What came from that experience was not the sophisticated, well-polished novel Hoagland had planned but a quirky, episodic series of character studies, cultural reportage, accounts of accounts and manner of their telling, conflicted recollections, and a vigorous but curiously elegiac narrative about the importance of narrative in defining place in the relentless river of time. Structured in the simple, plain-as-an-axe-handle form of a journal, *Notes from the Century Before* was published in 1969. It immediately established Hoagland not as the fiction writer he'd planned to become, but as one of America's finest essayists. The journal is still in print after almost forty years, its most recent edition released in 2002.

But the year before it first went to press, hoping to find new novel material to replace what he'd looted for the non-fiction book that hadn't yet made his reputation, Hoagland returned to the country he'd travelled two years earlier. He was, he said, escaping "a frenetic, sick nation, a national bewilderment," a country racked with tumultuous resistance to the Vietnam War, urban race riots, and the "Roman assassinations" of President John F. Kennedy, Martin Luther King, and Robert Kennedy.

Hoagland revisited his old-timers in the outback, recaptured old stories a second time, asked different people to tell the same story, found new stories, and, having won his informants' trust, was passed on to new storytellers.

The substance of those travels, like the intellectual artifacts accumulated by so many writers, didn't immediately find their way into anything, fiction or non-fiction. At the time, he felt dissatisfied with the results. But time has a way of changing the slant of light that gives shape and meaning to things. Now they've returned as *Early in the Season,* a literary extension of the earlier work that is somehow askew from the first book, altered perhaps, by the writer's own changing perceptions and circumstance. For example, on this second journey to the North, he leaves behind in New York and yet yearns to be with his new wife, Marion, five-months pregnant. The poignant reflections on imminent fatherhood and an urgency to domesticity that intrude into Hoagland's manly adventure journal provide a fascinating echo of Harmon's ruminations on the state of his own matrimony in the same place 140 years earlier.

Some of the language in this journal, replete with terms like "squaw" that are no longer acceptable in everyday speech, will offend some readers. But sometimes, as Hoagland observes in his essay "Small Silences," "we think we know too much about too much." The retroactive application of current social values to a journal that records the unmediated language of now-dead people whose attitudes are complicated, probably poorly understood even by themselves, and which we, thankfully, no longer share, seems a barren criticism and a disservice to the truth. Hoagland's journal is what it is: an honest narrative of a time and a place that really existed in all its simultaneous majesty and pettiness. Who's to condemn an unvarnished account that's faithful to the sometimes ornery, sometimes irascible, sometimes unlikable characters who tell their tales of wonder and disgrace.

Part of the journal's great value is that the good reporter, often without knowing, sees and reports what he doesn't see and thinks he never wrote about. In Hoagland's portrait of a former policeman with not much good to say of aboriginal people, what time uncovers is less an inherent racial prejudice than what appears to be fear. The character's attitudes look like an unconscious response to a new reality, the emerging political strength of tribal groups previously marginalized by mainstream society's self-justifying stereotypes, by a series of shattering epidemics that rent the cultural fabric, and by intolerably rapid economic change. Even as Hoagland jotted anecdotes about the "tough" Indians from the Nass Valley,

Chief Frank Calder and the Nisga'a Tribal Council were planning the court case that, in the following year, would forever transform the constitutional landscape for aboriginal rights in B.C.'s North.

But Hoagland's journals are not field notes for political scientists or sociology papers. They are stories shaped of flesh and blood that vividly capture the truth of their tellers, whatever embellishments, exaggerations, calumnies, or outright lies they might offer. Stories comprise the real substance of any place worth telling about, and if they are gathered and told by an outsider, from away, almost half a century later, so what? That world, already at the precarious edge of living memory when Hoagland encountered it, is gone. Now, thanks to that long-ago journey of literary self-discovery, it flickers back to life, resurrected for those of us who never noticed it disappearing.

Early in the Season

JUNE 6, 1968

Left New York on a smoggy but hot, cloudless day, from Kennedy Airport—this the day after Robert Kennedy's assassination. Everyone stupid with sorrow, poring over the papers or glued to the interminable radio commentary, and silent, no one telling others the latest "news," which is no pleasure to repeat in even the smallest of its particulars. The parting from my wife was doubly disconnected because of the discomforts of her pregnancy (beginning fifth month), though doctor yesterday said it was all right for me to leave. We're so very recently married that I haven't got used to using her name—say "my wife" instead of "Marion," though our beginning otherwise seems auspicious. The baby is wanted, now that our hasty, belated wedding is past, and we have love. We live in a quiet bit of Manhattan, at the eye of a hundred-mile hurricane of suburbs, etc., so that one begins by getting out of and above all this flux. I like living right at the hot centre, of course, but I'm also very tired of it. With the baby coming, I expect to be gone only a couple of months; that is our agreement, sealed after she chose to conceive. I'm tired physically and emotionally from an enormously productive spring, and I find, too, less of the boyish readiness that activated my travels to British Columbia two years ago. But the encouraging thing, if you read memoirs, journals, and such, is how very much people accomplish in a couple of months. This was true for some of the major explorers of the past like Mackenzie, as well as John Muir, and various eccentric side-figures like James Capen Adams, whose adventures I happened to read yesterday. Two concentrated months are potentially a long time. Whoever I see, whatever I write, I'll be exhausted by August. As usual, my plans are informal, except that they open up possibilities—as will fatherhood, next November!

Mostly today I'm transporting my body—and a good feeling too, to be getting away from the wretched redundancy, the cruel platitudes of the funereal. After Jack's death in 1963, I went to a Giants game I'd previously bought a ticket for, then walked one hundred eighty blocks home from the stadium. These Roman assassinations of ours. A frenetic, sick nation, a national bewilderment, and meanwhile the centurions of the status quo proclaim that more of the status quo—a more tightly cinched status quo—is the solution. We novelists are left in the shade by this surreality. Either *more* surreality, or a spare, clear art such as I lean towards, would seem to be the way to try to work it out.

Good flight. Over the Great Lakes, lots of clouds and a really white sun. Outer Edmonton—grey-black fields, as we land, cold air and cloud cover, remote-looking, empty and primitive; parking space downtown is five dollars a month. Farm faces, men's club medallions in the lapels. There's an Alberta mayoral convention at the hotel—greying hair, short alert figures.

JUNE 7

Edmonton is a new city with tall, pleasantly designed buildings, the streets all numbered in the one-hundreds (101 Avenue and 100 Street), the way some people like to number a new chequebook. I'm extremely tired, sleeping brokenly, and reading pornography, as I sometimes do after periods of accomplishment or hard work. It's a form of letdown. Melodic, moseying voices on the streets, gaunt girls, and the occasional dream-ridden Indian. Funny how suddenly loneliness comes on in a crowd, but my style of resting is to travel.

A five-hour train trip towards the heights of the Rockies. Great platform scenes—two kids seventeen having a fist fight, straight from the country—a *fist* fight! Little kids wave, wave, at the train. The prairie runs by in incremental mounds. The soil is black where it isn't green, as we roll through rain squalls, the train whining like a musical dog. People are travelling to visit their kin. A woman is reading aloud to her children, and outside some kids ride two-on-the-bare-back of a horse. It's mostly all forest after Edson, sparse Jack pine, poplar, and birch. Then the Front Range of the chockablock Rockies appears, and a wider corridor winding in. My seatmate tonight is a Norwegian railroader who retired a little ahead of the pension age because of asthma, after forty years work.

> Jeremy Hoagland stretched in the womb,
> Made his poor mother holler and croon.
> Jeremy Hoagland stuck out his fists
> And caused his dear momma to career and list!

JUNE 8

Canned orange juice and canned milk: tastes of the summer, I guess, and reminding me of my firefighting days in California fifteen years ago. The headlines have followed me here, however. The flags are at half-mast for Bobby Kennedy and people are telling me that they're sorry for me as an American. The murderer of Martin Luther King was captured today, in London, of all places. Of course there are always going to be those with an impulse towards martyrdom—a murderer's martyrdom—the notoriety and the rigid straightjacket of the law—people who long to be grasped and bound. Art in the past has been concerned with form. Now it involves the documentation of formlessness—ski jumps from the roofs of department stores and visionaries and glamorous personages murdered. Chaos and Brownian motion.

I'm at Maligne Lake, one of the showpiece lakes of the northern Rockies. My father and I stayed here in 1952. It was rather a bore for him because he didn't fish and he couldn't hike as I did; but afterward we took a three-day pack trip on horses with a half-tamed wolf running alongside. I found the tumbled skeleton of a bear that the wolf packs had killed on the mountainside and brought the skull home: also a dead eagle's feet, a set of elk antlers, and a mountain goat's horn which I found in a cave. It was all very real, indeed. Animals are becoming figures of speech, or educative symbols that children meet in their picture books. Although I don't like to confess it, my curiosity fails in regard to the future. I turn back from visualizing that life of mere spectatorship, watching the astronauts voyage, perhaps, and the Super Bowl game.

Maligne lies between rows of ten-thousand-foot mountains. The ice has just sunk into it this week. It doesn't melt or break up like the ice in the lower lakes; it gets pitted with holes like a honeycomb and simply sinks out of sight. I may make a practice of keeping a summer journal every year, during the time when I get off my ass and out in the woods and do some thinking. I am reminded of my father here. He's not actually as shadowy a figure as he appears to be in my books, and was nicer too, modest and conciliatory with others (and had Montaigne in his library).

You come into the bush early in the season like this and you feel a little spring rain on your face but you have the trails to yourself. I saw three moose, which with their legs hidden, looked like long-nosed wild boar with bleached manes. Also several deer, patches of whose fur had rubbed off after the winter. They have eyes like a rabbit, but they run like a llama. I talked to the Forestry Warden and he says the coyotes can kill them if they have gathered into a pack and can keep the deer out of a creek or a pool—deer can fight in the water, just as moose can. The wolves don't come through often, because these high narrow valleys, he says, don't give them the space and the meadows they want. Moose, caribou, and elk come up, however, and the moose stay in the high country even in winter unless they feel the snow belly-deep. He says that he goes on snow-shoes or on skis sleeved with skins for climbing, not with a sled, because the dogs (like wolves) need a more open, windswept type of country, and anyway the Service frowns on feeding your dogs Jasper Park moosemeat. He's lived alone for seven winters in this park.

"What do you learn?" I asked.

"You learn to put up with yourself. You learn to tolerate your own company," he said.

"Do you have hallucinations?"

"No. If you have hallucinations you get squirrelly, and if you're squirrelly, you can't tolerate your own company," he said.

JUNE 9

Dreamed about rabies, oddly enough.

Having just finished my wilderness book (*Notes from the Century Before*), I haven't a whole lot to say about these big vistas, but suffer from an author's temptation to revisit the scene of his crimes. The mountains look dramatic and incisive today. No sun, but a high ceiling, almost windless. I climbed in the Opal Hills, so-called, to the basin under the top ridge. Snow occasionally to my knees in drifts, otherwise gone. Saw some old black bear tracks on the path—hind foot the size of one of my hands. Very still today, woods quite empty, panorama on top, the lake green and white. I'm enjoying being alone, although thinking about New York literary politics, and the Kennedys, of course. Saw the tracks of a coyote and heard a short bark. Rubbed shoulders with some Maligne mosquitoes. Am glad to know I can climb to the places I climbed sixteen years ago, when I was nineteen. My reactions are quieter and smudgier, though, and the park is developing like Yellowstone. The tourists nowadays make comparisons of what they are seeing with the Hartz Mountains, or with Yucatan—they've been round the world. Usually this is the husband's summer. He takes his pictures and nibbles up facts. Next year the wife will take the family to Scotland or France.

If a person has just been married, like me, he kicks himself if his new wife isn't constantly in the front of his mind, when, as a matter of fact, it wouldn't be natural for her to be. The symbiosis comes with time. As it is, I think of how pretty Marion was in the three dresses she wore during the weekend of my sister's wedding. We marry for ambiguous reasons, most of us—partly because we're lonely, we've reached a dead end, we feel that we ought to have children already, or perhaps we're afraid of some unfathomable element in our makeup, such as homosexuality, or a more general malaise and panicky despair. It takes a few years for the marriage to rid itself of its beginnings. Two people thirty-five, gradually falling in love, who recognize some of their mistakes of the past and are sick of a sex life of fleeting affairs, start from a better position, but they still need to play it by ear.

I have two strengths in managing my personal life: my reluctance to act, avoidance of action when possible, and, on the other hand, my bee-lining directness if I do decide that the time is ripe. I was trained in the world of my gentle father, who never did battle with life, and yet, early on, I seized the principle of living to the hilt, of sampling it all, not shirking. Life is short; so I rise out of my fussy, cautious existence about once a year to *do* something.

JUNE 10

You know, as a matter of fact, I've thought once in a while of assassinating some figures myself: if not an enviably famous writer, then President Eisenhower or this President Johnson. I'm a romantic and a neurotic, and both play a part. It's the idea of at-a-stroke marking the world, remaking it, reversing history. And we've all had a lawless year. Right at the moment I'm liable for five years' imprisonment for my draft-card gesture! Me, a thirty-years goody-goody, who served in the Army. It's fundamentally this fantastically miscalculated war.

Passed close to my moose acquaintances again, two cows who keep company. Their humps wiggled as they trotted off. They forded the river, legs jutting at angles. The windfalls were so thick as I walked in the forest that it seemed a log fort had fallen down. Moss underfoot—the moss itself was the soil. In the breaks, no marmots but many ground squirrels. And wasteland areas—old rockslides, with marmots. There were footprints of coyotes and moose, though you couldn't tell when they were made. In the soggy June snow even fresh prints like my own don't look very crisp. Since the wolves of the spring are gone, there were no kills. On the steep slopes spruce replaced the lodgepole pine, which have a shallow root-net holding them up.

The heart is an accurate meter, registering every few degrees' change in the pitch of the land, but I was pleased to see how strongly I could still climb. I'm not as limber and tireless as a boy of nineteen, but I'm stronger, at thirty-five, which almost makes up for it. I did get a dim glimpse of the me who climbed for the same goal in 1952—fearless, an innocent, a rather good woodsman, and even more of an optimist than I am now. At that time I was convinced that no animal was going to hurt an animal-lover like me, not with the sixth sense I had. Now, while I'm eager enough to see grizzly tracks, I'd just as soon not see the bear himself. There's that fine line—wanting to be where he was *yesterday*. You try to walk loudly enough so as not to catch him by surprise, though not so loudly you won't see the other game.

After about four hours, I was up on the grand, goaty slope of Leah Mountain where I'd found the goat cave in 1952. Every small knoll was littered with droppings, and sometimes white tufts of hair. This manuring, and the southern exposure, has produced a luscious expanse of grass, but pitched at sixty or seventy degrees. It was slick where the snow was just off and there were intervals, equally slippery, of steep, shaley scree. Only one tree, with the top broken off; and spitting rocks bounded down, as fast as pitched balls from under my feet and also separately. I dislike tricky heights and had some scared moments. Then when I was coming around the corner of an escarpment, something stood up on the ledge just above. All very naturally, there was my neighbor, a bighorn ram. He possessed an immense, muscled neck, a neck as thick as my shoulders—a big wedge-shaped neck—and his ears were lost inside the circles of his huge horns. He was no laggard youngster; he was absolutely prime and heavy and grown. He wasn't twenty yards away, so I could see the cowlicks in his fur, and recognize that he'd give a wolf plenty of trouble. In fact, he was so unafraid I began to wish he were more afraid. It was like one of those sightings in a virgin valley. He was pushing his tongue in and out of his mouth, as a dog will do when prepared to fight, though this was not necessarily his reason. But, hearing my approach, he must have thought I was another sheep. Now, when he wasn't looking for a way up and out, he edged closer to me, magnificent in his musculature and posture, and more formidable than I could have imagined. He had that full heavy curl to his horns, as high as a helmet, a proper, unintellectual face, a Society face, except for the open, flat nostrils, and a clean, white hind end. I talked to him in a friendly voice, partly in hopes that he'd step back a bit. I had my own head thrown back, as one does when talking to somebody on a ladder. He was a living trophy; he was the finest bighorn, and surely the closest, I'll ever see; and yet I was the one who moved off first. He kept coming closer, and I had no trees to play monkey in, only a fall behind me, a drop-off, and my horns and my muscles were no match for his.

The goat cave would have been anticlimactic, if it hadn't been larger than I remembered. The rank smell announces it before you get there, and it has a sweeping, southerly view, good protection from the cold winds, and a grassy green promontory just in front. Smears of black dung go up the walls fifteen or twenty feet, where the goats clamber during the winter. There were some old bones of goats that didn't make it, much matted hair, and empty birds' nests in the limestone niches. One is the home of a furry-tailed rat who forages boldly among the goat droppings. He chewed for fleas in his white belly, watching me with his soft eyes while I ate my lunch, with more than a dozen mountains in sight. I remember in 1952 I saw a prowling wolverine from the same spot, and two annoyed eagles swooping at him, and I went to a higher valley which is full of boulders, so that it looks like a river of rock, and saw two wolves crossing.

JUNE 11

Not only am I not describing the peak-studded view which confronts you when you look down the lake—I don't look at it much. It's too stunning a sight to be useful. I wouldn't situate a character here because it's about as uncommon a scene as a table of ten movie stars would be, if you are a fellow who likes pretty women. The beauty is so concentrated, excessive, it is slapstick.

A cold cloudy day. Not being ambitious, I walked down the river a ways, doing a square dance routine between the dense pines, watching the skin of the current's wiggle, or looking up at the draped snowfields. You weave like a boxer and poke with your feet, or sometimes the moss on the forest floor gives way to cracked mud. There is a makeshift, provisional look to western rivers, with cutbanks like highway cuts. I saw five moose at varying distances. Ain't nawthin' to it, of course, in a National Park. They were like long-legged tapirs, carrying a gunbarrel body on giraffe legs. Also, to be perfectly frank, they look like horses at distances over a hundred yards. There's so much bullshit to wilderness books even people out here regard them as a bit of a dodge.

JUNE 12

Am reading Strindberg (*Inferno*), who is billed as Sweden's best writer; reminds me of Ingmar Bergman, whom I like better, I'm afraid. The visions, of course, are touching, though, and remind me of some of the torments of friends of mine who have fallen by the wayside. The point is that Strindberg didn't; he surmounted madness. But no writer's hindsight informs the descriptions with meaning— meaning for *me*—or explains why he *didn't* fall by the wayside. One reads simply with sympathy, therefore, not the terror that he intends, although his longing and guilty feelings about his first marriage do resemble my own.

Also read Evan S. Connell's *The Diary of a Rapist* (while the rest of North America was following the Kennedy funeral). The character is not a person, but much of the book is eloquent and first-rate—our lurid, Dickensian

violence, and no apparent way out. I want to write a story
set a few hundred years ago about a man who is going to
be stoned to death for a stutter like mine if he can't stop.

The success of a privateer's trip like this one depends
on its tone—the tone I maintain. And for a number of
possible reasons I'm not doing so well. Sudden, deleteri-
ous, nearly delirious spells of loneliness beset me, almost
send me home, make me change my plans three times in
an hour—whether to go promptly to the Yukon, or on to
Smithers and Hazelton, or back to Maligne Lake (because
of the young-thing hostesses), or maybe straight to an airport and East. Today I've come by train to Vanderhoof,
en route either to Hazelton or Manson Creek. My luck in
travel arrangements hasn't been awfully good, and each
small mishap sends my mood spinning. I haven't the
impetus of last time: the gaiety, the conviction. This is
a repeat. The most zestful old-timers, the best chunk of
country that was virgin, I may have already seen. And I've
just finished a new book, instead of being in that impel-
ling later state where one's last book has "failed" and one
is hunting for a new idea hard and fast to prove that one
is still a writer. I feel I may have done all I want to do
here, have wrapped it up, and have a hungering need for
women, too—I suppose it's that that makes me attractive
to them. I wouldn't survive a month without them (I don't
mean direct sex), yet last time, here in British Columbia, I
passed between them almost without interruption. Those
were great, spiritual, self-sustaining weeks!

I've got so many trips to remember. It's always a comfort in these between-book spells to submit to the rigidities of travel—the ironbound distances, the matter-of-fact courtesies and services purchased that make the world go round. This country is still empty, but the battle with it has been won. Our train crossed the brown, still rivers and quiet, subjugated miles of forest—old people from Nebraska and Manitoba with me and on tour. They're playful and rather gallant, like most of the old, but their faces are like day-old tapioca pudding; never a thought seems to have crossed their minds.

So the train makes a special stop for me at Vanderhoof. About 180 miles north of here by gravel road is Manson Creek, an old-timer's town. But the first people I asked didn't even know it existed, though that's the reason I'm here. Vanderhoof has a Chinese-owned restaurant, where newspapers are sold, a couple of five-and-dimes, "Smed's Auction Room," a couple of trucking warehouses, and one or two logging supply stores. The raw streets have 1930s cars, and big-brimmed hats, and barrel-chested, melodious-speaking, slow-mannered Indians with crusted boots and unwashed faces. People in winter coats, clodhopper boots, with beleaguered expressions. One burly apparition in his seventies—white hair to his shoulders, and a long beard—walks down the street, his head bent forward, with heavy momentum. That circle of hair is as big as an inner tube round his face, and he has prominent eyebrows and a straight forehead the complexion of beef. He's a prospector from Manson Creek, he says, so the place does await me, like a diamond mine, just as Telegraph Creek did two years ago, any time I want to go there.

First I went to the Senior Citizen's Home to talk to Tom Hamilton. Hamilton came to Canada in 1912 from Clay County, Kansas. The railroad ended at Tête Jaune Cache, and he continued by scow and raft to Fort George and homesteaded on the Stuart River, twenty miles off the nearest road. After World War 1 he farmed in Alberta awhile, married, came west to the homestead on the Stuart River again, then in 1943 went to work for a friend in Germansen Landing who had taken over the mine there from a New York millionaire. In 1949 he bought the trading post at Manson Creek from the Hudson's Bay Company and was the area's single storekeeper until 1963, when he sold out to two San Franciscans. He says the Hudson's Bay Company was systematically robbing the Indians there, as well as elsewhere, and only started closing up its outlying posts when the Indians became too smart to rob.

Tom is in his late seventies, his face whittled to the boniness of an Indian's. He talks about the mining: how they brought their water sometimes fourteen miles on flumes built of planks, or through ditches, then dammed it up and pumped it to the top of the tipple to build up water pressure for the five-inch monitor to shoot it like a cannon at the dry old creek bed and bust holes in the ground for the winch and buckets to lift material to the sluice box. He says that Manson Creek had only three feet of snow on the ground in the winter, but nearby you might find eight, ten, or twelve, on occasion. Originally the prospectors had arrived from the west by way of the Skeena River and Hazelton and the trails to Babine and Takla lakes. Other people came via the Crooked River to Finlay Forks and overland from the east. There were three characters in the middle period, about the 1930s, whom he says stood out in renown: Luke Fowler, a Chinese-Indian, carried the mail a couple of hundred miles overland from Hazelton to Manson Creek. Billy Steele had walked in in 1897, then didn't come out again for a peek at the outer world till 1938. He was the local mining recorder for the government, and died at eighty-three in Vanderhoof, having resisted being brought out to the hospital for fear he wouldn't be buried back in Manson Creek, where he had staked the meaningfulness of his life. The third was of course Skook Davidson, of wider fame, who still survives in the Kechika Valley.

I talked to Nat Porter, who works at the Vanderhoof Hotel. He was a Minnesotan, but came to British Columbia with his railroader family early in life, then trapped at the heart of the Parsnip River, and on the Nation River, and on the Omineca, and also prospected; later came to Manson Creek during the Depression to try to scratch out a living. We talked mainly about the Finlay River, however. He wandered around in that spacious country for a while, looking for nuggets that you could just pick up. Manson Creek was a come-on place, at the head of the supply trail, yet far enough off the beaten path so you could walk out and raise money on what you said you had found.

Fort Grahame, on the Finlay, had only eight or ten people, he says, plus a few transients, and a mica mine across the river. ("The only honest mine I knew of in the country.") Fort Ware had the few Sikanni Indians who remained around. And Shorty Webber lived at the Finlay Forks—as short and tubby as a beer barrel, a German national during World War I and therefore picked on, who later murdered his partner. There were also two German boys who were murdered for their furs and slipped through the ice. Skook Davidson was a great, big, big-hearted guy—but with your property as well as his own. He'd borrow your coat to give to someone else; or he'd borrow your horse and then have it die of a colic in the snow. He had a pack train and freighted to Manson Creek from Fort St. James. Later they used an old automobile dragging a string of sleighs (with a man in front feeling under the snow with a stick for the trail).

Nat Porter logged on the Omineca River, and worked at an open-pit placer-mine called "Germansen's Ventures," or made "soup" occasionally (homebrew). There was the post up at Finlay Forks and there was a "True Forks" on the Finlay too. Jake Fries, a two hundred-pounder, got sick with appendicitis (a "bellyache") one time but kept right on working, wouldn't lay down, till it burst on him and he doubled over. They carried him to bed, and his weight fell off to nothing in no time; he turned blue and red and finally died. Two of the guys meanwhile had walked to Hudson's Hope at the head of the Peace River for help, taking a couple of days, and a pilot, Ginger Cooks, therefore had flown in. But he hit the "waves" that the wind forms of snow on the ice, in landing, and broke a ski. He had to fix a new ski from green spruce quickly before any "rescuers" reached him (had no radio), however, or he would have had to pay for the "rescue." Everybody loves a "mercy mission"—both the money and the publicity—and Jake was already dead anyway.

Porter, hunting grizzly one spring, had had his sight knocked wrong against his pack board, although he didn't know it. He shot the bear five times to "call a halt" to his charge, but he wouldn't stay stopped. Finally the bear retreated, losing blood, up the mountainside, where Porter found that he had lain down waiting for him, looking down. Deep snow that Porter could hardly climb through. Never face a bear above you, or, even if he's dying, he'll roll down on you. So he left him alone. He would see groups of a dozen to twenty wolves in the winter; and mountain lions very occasionally came in from the coast via the Skeena River. Porter, now sixty-two, drove me, skidding and weaving on the gravel, the hour north to Fort St. James from Vanderhoof; then passed me

on, like everyone else always has, to who I *ought* to talk to.
I asked how many cabins he'd built for himself in his life.
He said not too many, maybe fifteen, maybe not as many
as that. There's always an old cabin somewhere near you
that you can fix up.

JUNE 13

In Fort St. James, a town of sneakered Indians and booted
whites, on Stuart Lake, I talked to Lee Cochran, a packer
and former Indian Bureau constable, and also to Harold
Smith and Bill Fraser (sixty-five and eighty-three). Fraser's
a thin, dry but kindly guy; Smith, short and hefty. Both
were fur traders and freighters, Fraser for the Hudson's
Bay. He came from Scotland to New York to Telegraph
Creek in 1908, but left there in 1919 to manage the store
down here, two weeks' walk southeast. He was the one
who used to entertain Luke Fowler at the end of his two-
hundred-mile mail run, sledding from Hazelton. His
wife had learned to cook from Frank Jap. Now she walks
leaning on a metal frame. Harold Smith was meanwhile
a competitor of the Hudson's Bay Company, working
for the Takla Trading Company, on a lake halfway back
towards Hazelton.

But Billy Steele was king of the Manson Creek area,
they say. He was the mining recorder and then when
each little outfit duly folded, he'd appropriate its grub and
equipment for his personal use. Yet he was always hungry.

He had a five-hundred-pound cookstove in his cabin that had been brought from Ashcroft, using tripods to pack it on the back of some poor mule. Also had a huge, flowered mirror that he'd salvaged from a ghost-town saloon. He could talk the Indian languages, as well as mimic them well. Billy Steele was around Manson Creek from the age of seventeen to eighty-three, and mined on Slate Creek himself. He married Indian girls several times, but finally would kick them out when their sundry relatives came and moved in, as they invariably did. Had an ornery tongue, and several times took a gun to the Indians. He had three dogs and lived so filthy that the blankets on his bed looked as if they were actually made of dog hair. Besides Slate Creek, he worked on Luck Creek, which was named for Sun Luck, a "Chinaman" miner of olden days. For all his finagling, Billy never made more than just enough to feed himself, and not very well by the standards of anybody living outside of the bush. He was on the downhill skids already by World War 1.

Now, Fred Aslin, of the Burns Lake region later, was a great winter hiker. He would go from Babine Lake all the way to the Bella Coola country on snowshoes, a ten-day walk. He was "a squaw man one hundred per cent," and ostracized for it. He weighed only 140 pounds, but, boy, there was a lot of it, because he loved to fight. Hard to understand at the table, because he chewed a lot of corn mush when he talked. But he travelled on dried salmon because it was light to pack and expands in the pot, or in the stomach, and he sure "knew the raw gold when he saw it," says Lee Cochran, the former Indian Bureau policeman.

Luke Fowler had a claim on Blackjack Creek, where he just about made enough to eat. But he used to walk from Hazelton to Fort St. James or vice versa with mail or messages. Point him in the right direction, and give him something to spend when he got there, and he'd go. He used to study the stars and say what he thought was behind them. Rarely stopped along the way when he was travelling, except to eat his fish and rice and tea. Or he'd used to tie up hotcakes on a string between two trees, and let them freeze, and have them there to eat on the trip home. If he came across the old bones of a moose that somebody had killed in the snow, he'd boil up soup—boil out the germs and the smell and boil the marrow out of the bone. He painted his cheeks red (being a Chinese-Indian, "a Hazelton half-breed," according to Cochran), and he grew his hair to his waist, just like a brave or like a woman. He practised as a medicine man, making more money that way than on his actual claim.

Jimmy Alexander, a strapping six-footer, "about a half-breed," Cochran tells me, freighted on the riverboats clear down to Quesnel. Ended operating a government ferry on the Fraser. He'd walked in from Winnipeg, taking six months to do it, and accompanied Frank Swannell, who first surveyed the Finlay River. He was like a bear in the bush. Five or ten miles meant simply nothing to him—a matter of an hour or two—travelling always at a jog, living on the grouse, moose, bobcat, or Dolly Varden he got. Went ninety miles nonstop in a day, with the mail, to Fort McLeod, or way north to the Ingenika River, on snowshoes—not bothering with dogs. Died at ninety.

Some of the Indians were "awfully miserable," though. On Cochran's regular rounds, he might meet a whole family huddled around a campfire in February, but tent-less, and simply following a fisher's track, to catch and sell the eventual fur. Thomas Abraham, a tall Bear Lake Indian, used to travel with his family in tow, but the children and the women carrying thirty to seventy pounds of property apiece, and their dozen dogs so overloaded that you'd meet them staggering, or lying splayed out on the trail behind, waiting to creep into camp finally that night. And Abraham walked in front, choosing the path, and car-rying only his gun. His wife, however, used to ride their brown horse in the summer, with an umbrella cocked over her head. Cochran—then the constable—suspected the Abraham "outfit" of having murdered a couple of white men who went up into that Bear Lake country alone at different times. It was halfway to Telegraph Creek, and he says that although in Fort St. James they seemed innocu-ous enough, if you met them on the trail "they'd as soon kill you as look at you." Says, "There's nothin' much to tell about *him* except he was a dirty bugger." It was outlaw country up there, and although for several years the government had closed the beaver season, Thomas Abraham kept right on trapping, and secretly hung the skins where they kept nice and dry. And when it got to be legal again to sell them, he sold six thousand dollars worth and held a potlatch at Babine Lake—about the last of the great potlatches before the government outlawed those. Officially, the potlatch was to reward the other Indian bands—not blood relations—who had come in during the previous year and buried somebody of consequence from the home band, who themselves weren't supposed to handle the body. But this one was very big. A hundred-fifty came over from Hazelton and from Kispiox Village, alone, and some came south scores and scores of miles from the Stikine River, plus the Bear Lake Indians themselves, and the Kitchener Lake and Klappan River bands, as well as the Takla Lakers; and Simon Gunanoot, the famous Skeena River fugitive, showed up. Indians from thousands of square miles all around, and just great heaps of sacked sugar and flour and rice lay on the ground to be given out. There was naturally a dance. It was all located on Hudson's Bay Company land, but Harold Smith and his Takla employer also went down in a scow, which they anchored in the Babine River just offshore, and traded there, in order to compete.

They used to scow to the head of Takla Lake and pack overland to their subsidiary post on Bear Lake, with thirty to forty horses. Sometimes they had to buy back from the Indians horses they'd sold to them earlier for "four to five times" what would be one's proper price (about twenty-five dollars), and complain about the Indians taking "the Jew's one per cent." A Prussian kept the Bear Lake store for maybe six years, and he knew how to handle Indians— "knock 'em down and only talk to them later." When Cochran, who dislikes Indians, started out as a constable, they were looking to bluff him and get him on the run. But he had been a P.T. instructor in the army, so he could fight in spite of his short height; and, "white or black," whatever the man was, he'd fight him. (City men he calls Hoosiers, for some reason.)

Archie King came down with a case of quinsy on his Ingenika River claim, he tells me, continuing, and two of his buddies tried to sled him out of there in the deep snow, before he died. If it had stayed cold, they might have been all right, but a soft spell of weather came on, and they were floundering to make half a mile in an hour, wearing themselves out in no time. So he died. They'd run out of food already and they were starving, so they hung Archie up in a tree to keep the wolves from grabbing him and made a dash south for Takla Landing to get food. Frank Johnson was another old-timer who came to an unfortunate end. He had been another phenomenal walker. His dog could hardly keep up with him. But one day he disappeared some place in the headwaters area of Manson

Creek. His dog came back with a nose full of quills, a day later. So then they stupidly shot the dog. But that meant they didn't even have the dog to lead them back to wherever Frank Johnson was.

Since he's been crippled up, the legendary Skook Davidson hunts on horseback for moose, but won't let anyone else shoot within ten miles of his cabin, so that the mountain sheep come right down in the winter to feed. His treatment for a stomach ailment is no food or water for one day, and no food the next, but maybe a little water. He has lost the use of his legs; just uses his sharp hands to ride his "tom-horse," or "stud-horse." "Skookum" means "tough" in Indian. Skook was turned down once by a girl in Dawson Creek, when he proposed, so he sent her a rocking chair as a pointed present. Another time, he chartered a plane to go and see her, but so many of his friends wanted to go along that they filled up the plane and he sent them ahead without him. When Skook did come into town, the kids would pour out, shouting, "Skook's here! Skook's got back!"—because he gave them candy and so on. The Indians liked him, but he "kept them in their place," Cochran says approvingly. He'd pack out two-hundred- to three-hundred-pound bales of beaver fur from Babine Lake, after bringing in boxes of food. That was his profession, and he rode a white mule for years, and sometimes would rein it right into a bar and order up a drink for it as well as himself. Whenever he took a drink he'd rub the last few drops into his hair to keep it growing good—keep from going bald. He bought bags of sugar every fall especially for his old horses, too, his "pensioners," to give each of them a handful at nightfall. Though really just a drunken bum in town—as opposed to out on the trail, where he worked rough-and-tough—he always looked after his horses, even there. And had medals from World War 1, but wouldn't talk about them. Being a big spender with his own or other people's money, he was always popular, though he rode off for the Kechika River at last to settle down with some horses that weren't actually his, in retirement. Now only Gunanoot, the great, dead Gitksan outlaw, rivals Skook as a topic of nostalgia. And Skook is alive.

JUNE 14

These guys who are coy and grinning when talking to me, or else just frankly mum—serious, unsmiling, doubt-ful, unamused—once I mention a name like Billy Steele's or Skook's, their faces break the poker pattern and look affectionately wistful and kind. I read for a while on the water landing beside the two dilapidated sawmills, which squeaked and rumbled. Fort St. James is a very pleasant town physically, open and historical, with the wide, long, pretty lake, and settlements of Swedes and Estonians that have been abandoned along the sides. There is more meanness here than in Telegraph Creek, however, more mockery of the Indians and money-making scheming, more summer visitors, and not the same self-contained effervescence of that remote spot. But it's another gold mine of lore, and these people are the real thing, real pros in the bush, compared to the Colorado cowboys I met last summer in Aspen.

Lee Cochran was a packer, like Skook, mainly, and joined the police force when trucks replaced horse pack trains. He's a diminutive, combative fellow, and says the real trouble with Shorty Webber, the placer miner murdered on the Finlay after being a murderer himself, was that he "always pulled for the Indians," and not necessarily from the goodness of his heart, but because he had a little store and profited by it. He got in charity clothes for them from Vancouver—girdles and brassieres on the Finlay River! Cochran launches into regular tirades on the subject of the Indians ("I wish *I* was on the Indian rolls!"). Says their language is filthy, they're half-dressed, out on the street: Welfare, welfare, welfare. Will sell their very groceries for liquor. Describes how the old Indian agents used to beat the living shit out of them—stop 'em on the road and beat 'em. None of this genteel Mountie-handling, wrestling them into the cop car. And he says squawmen ought to be chopped up in little pieces with tomahawks. Describes finding a freezing little girl in the snow and bringing her into his *garage* to thaw, not to the house, because she was an Indian. He was a policeman for

the ten post-World War II years. Before that, he packed
at Barkerville and at Stewart—at the Salmon Gold Mine
and the Big Missouri Mine. There was thirty feet of snow
on the ground, one time. Five feet fell in one night, but
it was heavy, wet, coastal snow which hardened quickly
on the trail. The horses wore snowshoes—round steel
frames with mesh webbing, and they got so picky that
they wouldn't go out of the barn without these on.

George Byrnes at Hazelton tried to hire Cochran to
pack on the Telegraph Trail for 150 dollars a month, but
he came here and packed to Thutade Lake and Bear Lake
and the Ingenika River instead, swimming the floods in
the spring—lots of adventure for a youngster. The "storekeeper" whom he delivered to was usually just an ordinary prospector on the scene, who'd keep an extra ton
of supplies around to sell to the Indians and to passersby.
The prospectors, as he says, "didn't have much trouble carrying out what gold they'd got at the end of the season. So
you only packed once for them: at the beginning, in the
spring." Gunanoot, he claims, holed up for two winters
successfully with the prospector who lived at McConnell
Creek. And one packer used "clooches" instead of horses
to carry his stuff east from Hazelton, paying them collec-
tively ten cents a pound, and giving the leader-woman a
list of what there ought to be at the other end, to hand
over to the trader to check. They called her "the bell
mare," and she was dependable.

Cochran and his buddies on the trail used to crawl under a huge tarpaulin together to go to sleep and escape the mosquitoes, since they had no bug juice or bug netting, lying under that with just the corners propped up slightly with four sticks. Some of the large rivers held the wolves back in the summer, because they don't like dangerous swims, until the ice let them cross again in the fall. When World War I came along and the country was emptied of people, they migrated down from the north and their numbers increased, till the trappers returned. Muskeg isn't too dangerous for one trip—the horses pussyfoot across that particular stretch—as long as the grass isn't chopped up by the hoofs of many trips before, and as long as there are roots to the tussocks. If you keep some of your horses belled, the grizzlies are warned away from the pack train. The likeliest time you may blunder across a bear is in the morning, when you're out hunting your horses in a brushy valley. But once, after an early deep snowstorm in September, he had to shoot eleven—out of forty-eight—starving horses, coming home from Thutade Lake, but trapped under Sustut Peak for several days.

ALBERT ALEXANDER is the son of Billy Steele and Agate Alexander, who was called the Omineca River Queen. She had lived with other white men and with an Indian husband, name of Louie. She was a match for any man at working, walking, trapping fur, felling trees, or going out to find and rescue someone. She was a breadwinner, but Billy taught Albert how to write his name and speak a little English. Many of the Indians here look like Hades' creatures, however. They have bleached skin, with a Mongol shape to the face below it, and wear iridescent windbreakers and white blue jeans. But huge puffy heads on some of the children, alas, and bruises and cuts and discolourations, half-hidden by long black hair. Staring, zombie-like older Indians with washed-out, bleached-out faces sit about, with just a ghost of the "Indian" left, or like a degenerated, skimmed-down white man. Yet there's only a small group of old-timers left in this Stuart Lake country—a one hundred-year-old Indian died just last year, and Fred Aslin and Agate Alexander the year before that, and now Bob Watson is dying and also another guy. You cross the names off your list of the old-timers, who it turns out are already dead or are incoherent or comatose.

Alex Rosen, though, came in from Hazelton thirty-seven years ago. He's a Jew with a Swedish accent—one side of his face crumpled up, with a glass eye in it, watering, and part of his ear missing, which he keeps turned away. He lost the eye in the First War, and a couple of other pieces of him too, and (or so he says) when he got back he simply "took to the woods." Now his heart has gone bum on him; it goes haywire and he's got to sit down, but after a little rest he can putter around. After working on the coast, he was in my beloved Telegraph

Creek for the gold strike of 1924, on a tributary of the
Eagle River—which flows into the Dease—which flows
into the Liard. But that didn't amount to much. He got
a little bit of gold and then sold out to a local guy after
a couple of summers. Then he came here eventually, in
1931, after hearing about the new strike on Rainbow
Creek. There were colder winters and warmer summers
then. He was too late to stake any real sort of a claim for
himself, so he worked for a man named Snell, a farmer,
and they found a few flakes of gold in the black sand, but
nothing much. Later he made a small strike of his own,
but threw it up when the day's payoff fell too low—the
ups and downs of mining. He also prospected a bit on
Pelly Creek, which parallels the Finlay, going close to
Fort Ware. But the group of them who were doing it
came down from there on the freight boat finally, giving
up. It was a wide, limestone valley with plenty of moose
and lots of bear. They carried fly dope and rifles, because
bears aren't like dogs that sniff around and walk away. A
black bear wants to investigate and chew on everything
and pull down the tents, though what he mostly eats in
midsummer is grasshoppers. They didn't look much at
the country. Mostly they walked through in a businesslike way, rafting back and forth across Pelly Creek when
they had to, which is fifty yards wide, just looking at the
rocks, and then throwing them away, since they weren't
mineralized.

This is a sprawled out, messy sort of town geographically. I've got to do a lot of walking between the houses, which is fine. I'm feeling glad and peppy, delighted I'm here.

The white old-timers either started out as prospectors or as Hudson's Bay Company men, buying furs from the Indians and selling supplies. L.R. Dickinson had his own store, however, starting in 1916. He'd come in five years before, as a surveyor's helper with my friend of two years ago, Frank Swannell, after having grown up in the Fox River country in Wisconsin. He's a penetrating, gentle-hearted businessman with dusty glasses—a benefactor to the locals, after the pattern of the Sargents in Hazelton and of Steele Hyland in Eddontenajon. He lives extremely modestly in a cottage, and has his office in a shack that is fifty years old but that he uses as a warehouse, so he never manages to empty it long enough to tear it down. This was Saturday afternoon, and as we talked a regular procession of Indians came in to borrow five bucks for the weekend from him, sometimes for the beer hall, but with the reason given that the fellow was going fishing and needed gas for his outboard motor, or needed bus fare for his daughter to go to a picnic. Another woman came in with eight twenties, towards paying off what she owes.

"That's the way it is in this country. The money comes in in bunches; it don't come in in nickels and dimes." (It's such a balm to be here with the peaceful Canadians!

They're my escape hatch on this rancid, tumultuous continent.) He remembers Jimmy Alexander as a raw-boned, husky man, more in the pattern of an eastern Indian, and the son of a Hudson's Bay man, who later went out and had a separate, white family in Prince Rupert. Jimmy was "docile" unless provoked, but then would poke a fellow in the jaw. The Indians resented him because he was a "half-breed" and, if he was drunk enough, they would beat him up. Dickinson only got to know Luke Fowler in his dying days. Luke had cooked for the Okerson & Dagineau outfit, when an old man. Luke, with his weather forecasts, used to say, when the weather was dry, that "there is only half an inch of water left in the sun—it's going to boil dry." He often joked, but kept a straight face.

Fred Aslin had been married to a white woman in Stewart, until they separated, and he left her with the store there and came over here and traded at the post on Babine Lake. "Married" a squaw and had a big family. Skook Davidson, he says, "is pretty well used up now." He was a man of principle but he had a dangerous sense of humour—"he'd practically hang you if he thought there was a joke in it." He didn't know what fear was. He'd walk towards an Indian who had a .30-30 pointed at his gut. He was a hard man—could just live on practically nothing—yet a man of principle in the sense that his pack horses never had sore backs, and that before he went on a bender, he'd hire a boy to look after them.

A claim cost thirty dollars a year rental from the government, and then one hundred a year in assessments had to be paid. One man could stake up to eight claims, if he could pay the fees. Dickinson bought his own claim from a consumptive fellow who needed money to get to the sanitarium. There were blind-piggers (bootleggers) and poker-players in the country, too. You couldn't associate with them socially, but you could trust them; their word meant what they said, then. You could hand them 150 dollars and get it back next Saturday night. For instance, Cap Hood, who was from the Yukon gold rushes (called Cap because he'd sometimes run scows up there)—he'd had gambling clubs along the British Columbia coast, and was always chewing tobacco. He'd reach into his pocket for a plug during the game, which was useful because he had a deft and capacious hand that sometimes he'd pull a pair of aces from, if he needed them. Poker's too cold-blooded a game to play with friends, says Mr. Dickinson. You're just trying to take the other man.

He says that "you can live among the Indians but you can't live with them. They move in, they ask a hundred favours; they have no sense of holding back." There are eight hundred around this Stuart Lake. It's a communal culture, foreign to nuclear-family whites. He says that Cochran talked tough with them but did them neither good nor harm, in effect, whereas *his* job, of course, was to protect them from scammers and do them good. In the old days, half of them used to die in infancy and the women wore shawls and carried their babies everywhere on their backs. A few guys would come in and try to cheat them—here today and gone tomorrow—give them a phony "cheque" for their furs. The real businessmen in town would shun these fellows and tell the Indians they were bad. The Hudson's Bay was "here before the white men," the Indians used to say, and on Dominion Day, July 1, the semi-outlaw Bear Lake band would come in for a spree and to sell their year's furs. Merchants like Dickinson would set up a few prizes for their contests, such as the tug-of-war between the women of different bands. There was Peter Himadam, the brother-in-law of Gunanoot, a chesty fellow, but who "lost his mental balance" when he drank. The Hudson's Bay men were often itinerant fur traders who took on a post in order to settle down for a while and raise a family.

Dickinson likes to use the phrase "several years ago," meaning twenty or thirty or more, and he tries to speak fairly well of everybody, but not like Johnny the Jew, who never criticized anybody—not even Shorty Webber, the murderer whom he lived with on the Finlay. He worked as a watchman later on at the mill here, and prospected again, and was an expert fly fisherman, and accurate in talking—"If it was nine it was nine, it wasn't ten." In the early years of the century people were either settling or pretending to but speculating, making a down payment of twenty-five cents per acre. The full price from the Canadian government was two dollars and fifty cents an acre. Of course the first 160 acres—a "quarter"—was free. Then buying three more quarters to add to this homestead made a "section," which is what everybody wanted. But, with World War 1, the economics of the frontier fell flat and a lot of people lost their down payment. In town, or "the Fort," two areas developed, "the townsite," for whites, and "the reserve," for Indians.

JUNE 16

Young adventurous geology crewmen and surveyors are in town, en route to the bush, putting in the glory years they will remember. With some of these old-timers, it's a little like seducing a girl to get them to talk to you. They *want* to, but they don't want to. The tradition here is to be modest and taciturn, so they think they oughtn't to, and there's been so much bullshit told and written that they haven't much respect for the written word—between the boasters and braggarts and grizzly pulp writers. Yet at the same time they know this will be the only way of preserving a personal history. I dangle my map in front of them like bait—ask them first just to describe a particular river for me, so they won't draw back. Also my previous travels northwest of this area, to Hyland Post, Atlin, and Telegraph Creek. Or I'll use one of the key names, like Skook's, and watch that irresistible smile spread across their faces. They've drawn back and bridled at first, but then they put on a studying expression and begin to talk. I huff and I puff with my terrible stutter, and that may help, too, because handicapped people have a history of being quite effective here. And since I can't talk, *they* do. Just like the circus was in the 1950s, this frontier country is a place where misfits have gathered, and they are likely to accept my problem as brotherly.

The old Indians aren't so coy, however; they're natural and hearty. John Prince is eighty-two, and he used to carry the mail to Finlay Forks for eight years every month, a three-week round trip for a couple hundred dollars. He had a toboggan and several sled dogs (pack horses during the summer), and would pick up extra money packing grub for the trappers and several placer miners too. When the river opened up and the mail went in briefly on boats, he'd work on somebody's claim or keep carrying in food. He'd stay with Billy Steele, en route. Then he had a store at Chuchi Lake, on the Nation River, but went broke, and worked on the steamboat at Quesnel, down on the Fraser, for a dollar twenty-five a day. (You could buy a bottle of Hudson's Bay rum for that. Now it's seven dollars, he says.) Or he'd trade a bear hide for six dollars worth of grub at the Hudson's Bay, and travelled round for Hudson's Bay buying marten and fox. He says Thomas Abraham, once so scary to whites and formidable, died in the TB hospital in Prince Rupert, and Peter Himadam was shot in Hazelton by a crazy Indian, who'd just shot a woman also, and then ran off into the bush like a bigfoot and shot himself.

"Billy Steele died long time ago, you know," he says. "He didn't die rich; he died poor. The Indians liked him. Lots of bullshit stories; and he drink too, you know. And he buy furs from Indians in the middle of the winter, when they running low and sell to him for grub. Indians good then. Now steal, drunk all the time, break into stores, shoot people," John Prince says. "Everybody likes me, especially whites. I never crooked." One of his sons was killed in World War II, in Italy. The other seven kids have also died by now. "All alone now." Goes to all three masses at church on Sundays, collects the collection, getting ready to die. "Priest couldn't get along—wouldn't hold the service—without me."

He has one glassy blue eye, not functioning, and his ears lie back close to his head. Has a huge head, close-cut hair, glasses shining. A stiff, blown-out torso; cheerful, deep-cut face. And keeps saying, "He died, you know. Yes, he died. I think he maybe had cancer." Schooling, he says, has wiped out the old Indian stories. The kids don't know them, and he has forgot. He used to know a long, long story he'd like to tell me. He says a caribou in the winter can put its nose down and smell when a snowslide is coming and run back—the rest of the herd is waiting, in the meantime, in the trees. And a beaver knows how hard the winter's going to be. "He cuts lots of sticks for hard one—you go out and see." And, "There are lots of wolves again. Indians aren't trapping them—I don't know what they going to do." He ends the interview by closing his eyes, yawning, and saying he hasn't had his breakfast.

Alex Leggatt is a shiny-skinned, long-faced fellow, quick and precise in his motions; no wasted energy at all. A saw-filer in a mill till his health went bad; decided to get outdoors for the sake of his lungs. Lived in a big house-cabin during the Hungry Thirties and carved tree burls for decorations. Lost the ends of his fingers at that. Came into this country in 1940. Had a sawmill, and then took two years vacation-with-pay as a POW of the Germans during World War II. Did lots of prospecting thereafter, both on salary for Kennecott Copper and on his own, on the Mesilinka and the Osilinka rivers, and in the Omineca country, as well. He prospected for himself in the summer and mined at Kitimat in the winter, on their payroll then. He says when you're on your own in the bush you've got to be careful not to take it too easy. You've got to get yourself up and out by 8 AM and not come back till 5 PM, just like a business, because it's awfully boring when you're not finding too much.

Alex Rosen was his partner for a while. Rosen was older, so Leggatt did the climbing and Rosen covered the lower country, like a man with a weak heart. They didn't even pack a rifle that trip. Rosen was the fisherman, and he'd simply say to Leggatt, who was the cook, "How many fish do you want? Two apiece, three apiece?" They camped at an unnamed ten-acre lake where all you had to do was drop the line in and you'd catch a thirteen-inch char: No other size and nothing else. The wolves came after each suppertime to pick up the leavings—they'd cleaned the fish beside the lake. And the groundhogs down along the valley would whistle the wolves in, signaling their gradual progress, and their wandering departure afterwards. Leggatt fed hotcakes to a couple of groundhogs, right in camp—would cook extra—until finally these ones grew to be just like butterballs. They had an ore sack with a thirty-foot rope tied to the mouth, to put their meat in and hang it in a tree, because bears usually don't smell food high up. But the trees at that altitude were pretty low, and the bears got some of it anyway. They'd had rubber mattresses and a sheet of plastic over them, for shelter, but the bears ripped these up.

"If they can't use it themselves, they want to make damn sure nobody else is going to use it."

This was open country, not tight—not those V valleys a fast river can cut. They let the claim drop, but now they have picked it up again—he, and two partners, and some Vancouver man who put in 25,000 dollars. They're bringing in a diamond drill, and they've each given themselves 65,000 shares, Leggatt says.

He tells me people resent the current Takla Landing trader a little bit for introducing leathercraft among the

Driftwood Valley natives (he'd previously taught some Eskimos, at his last post), because they're shooting a lot of moose for the hides. These jackets turn practically to mush when rained on, just like suede does, until they get stiff with your body oils and from having grease rubbed into them. His best summer was in 1950, he says, when he went up the Finlay River in the freight boat, altogether a five-day trip. The river is about 125 feet wide. Fort Grahame had closed in 1949, so the Indians there had moved either up the Ingenika or else to Fort Ware.

They met Skook at Fort Ware, who'd brought nine horses with him and went on to the Toodoggone River (pronounced Toodeegone), although Skook even back then had to ride side-saddle, he was so stiffened up from arthritis, and mounted by means of a wooden box. Yet he jumped on nevertheless and swam the horses across the Finlay, when no one else dared. The years of wet work and sleeping on wet ground had probably done it to him, although he used to try to put his age ahead and pretend he was older than he really was, Leggatt says. He'd got an army pilot to fly them in a case of rum, while they waited for supplies. They'd crossed at Ware and took the short cut at Cutoff Creek and McConnell Pass, recrossed the Finlay at Fishing Lakes, building a raft to get their ton of supplies over. Reef Canyon and Kodak Cataract was below, so they had to pull the raft carefully upstream each time they crossed. Then they were in lovely high country all that summer. Pulpit Lake and Katherine Creek. Lots of caribou, little ones, eighty-five pounds of meat on each, when butchered. You could throw the whole thing over your shoulder, yet make it last for two weeks. They sometimes smoked it, in net or canvas bags. But if they accidentally made a cut into fresh meat, a blowfly would go into the hole and ruin the rest. The caribou were in herds of twenty-five or thirty, and if you were on a horse you could ride straight into the centre of a group and pick your animal without frightening the remainder until you shot it. They didn't bother with moose, however, because the moose were too big to eat.

The Caribou Hide band of Indians had been moved to Telegraph Creek in a previous year, but some beaver trappers had been back that spring and written their names on a tree at the deserted village of Caribou Hide. Maybe thirty houses remained, and some of them board houses, too, because a placer outfit had moved in and out a few years before and set up a defunct white-man's sawmill. But once they got up and away from the spruce trees and underbrush, they saw acres of flowers, lupine and fireweed and pea vine and grass, a whole garden of the world. Geese Creek, the Frog River, and the Chukachida in a wide valley, and a big, bald-headed, loaf-shaped mountain, westerly, to which they climbed to look down upon my Hyland Post.

I like Strindberg's *Alone,* Melville's *Alone,* Thoreau's *Alone*—in fact all of the ways of being successfully

Alone—and can see myself probably dying like my father did, last June, with an accepting though ironic smile, braced for a last adventure, and at the same time thinking that it's not so special: now it's my turn. This evening I waited an hour on Jack Thompson's stoop. We had an appointment. He's a bald, black-Irish squaw-man who lives in a battered one-room shack behind the gas station. Yet even in the gas station they don't know who he is. He's a nice enough guy, though, and after I'd stuttered to him for a minute (he didn't understand a word I said), he offered me a ride to Manson Creek in the back of his pickup. That's where the dogs ride. And happy dogs they are, too.

JUNE 17

But instead I'm in Hazelton again! It's a town steeped with memories of my previous wife and therefore bittersweet for me because we were happy here in 1960. In the evening sunlight, with the mid-June grass up to my knees, the trees full-leaved, and the luscious, huge Skeena River hustling past, noisy as a narrow ocean, and the horses hock-deep in the river drinking, the mountainsides still swashed with snow, it's just about the loveliest town I'll ever see anywhere at all. Steep short roads, log cabins eighty years old, and the happiest childhoods that anyone is spending from here to Hannibal, Missouri—Chinese, Indian, and towhead kids. I went up on the hill by the graveyard and

felt the most exhilarated—sheer exultancy—that I've felt
for weeks, weeks, and weeks.

Hazelton is no ghost town, like Atlin, and yet it's not
strewn about in a hodgepodge manner, like Fort St. James.
The old town is protected by its encircling Indian reserve.
Of course, it is hooked into the contemporary world by
the Canadian National Railways, as Telegraph Creek, my
favourite, is not; but generally it's got the best of all worlds.
And there's a brutalized tone to life in Alaska, for instance,
an air of rapine, which seems to be creeping into life in
British Columbia as well—but the Hazelton enclave has
kept that out. The old-timers are dead, however. Apparently there's almost no one left for me to talk to, in contrast to Fort St. James and Telegraph Creek. This was the
oldest of those three towns, the first to be developed, and
so its old-timers were the oldest, too.

The bus trip was all scenery still. You look out through
the mud on the windows at the eternal road-grading
going on, the cut-up roadsides, the cat-slashed, torn-up
woods, but fifty miles of forest between towns, and hun-
dreds of miles extending to the north. Every bar has
separate Ladies' and Men's entrances. I was wearing the
shoes, socks, and a coat of my dead father's, and once in
a while, at a coffee shop or what not, a desolately lonely
feeling came over me, even a feeling of needing to "fill"
the summer up, so as not to go back to Marion early with
my tail between my legs. Delight and pride in covering

ground is one of the heritages of the frontier, but at the lunch stop every book in the paperback rack was a murder mystery, or *Backstage Nurse,* or *Nurse of the North.* I remember, as a matter of fact, in Hazelton eight years ago, a girl tried to seduce me. She wasn't a nurse but was a nursing mother, and that fact about her did attract me, as attracted to breasts as I am. The fact that men don't have them is one of the reasons I didn't become homosexual, when I had the choice to make.

JUNE 18

Talked to Mr. Sargent this morning, a kind and haunted-looking man of fifty-three whose father founded the principal store in town, after being a Hudson's Bay man here for ten previous years. He's soft spoken, sweet-natured, and bright. His wife is currently the mayor and mover and shaker of Hazelton, a good, busy woman readying a costume celebration for Dominion Day. He says he's gone out of the fur-buying business because most of the Indians have stopped trapping, and anyway they charged him, or he paid, the same price for furs as he could later charge. He says he'd overgrade the furs when buying them, for the Indians' sake, and then the Greek fur merchants in Vancouver would undergrade them when they bought from him, so he wasn't making anything. There was a pent-up, post–World War II boom in furs, when people wanted luxuries, but then the Siberian and Chinese furs hit the market, knocking the bottom out.

He says that history is disappearing. There's a great confusion now between the different Telegraph Trail line cabins, and the halfway cabins between them, for instance, and even the lost village of Kuldo's location. Kuldo is "ephemeral," he says, not identifiable now. It appears from the air and disappears, but seems to have been a year-round settlement, not just a summer hunting camp, for two or three families—throwbacks and eccentrics who lived very primitively. His father once made a list of people who wintered there, ending with "and two Chinamen." He remembers Ritch Leland, a British veteran of the Boer War. And he remembers, as a child, Cataline, the famous Telegraph Trail packer—aquiline face, long grey hair, a black frock coat, and the shirt for a detachable collar (only no collar)—a powerful, short man with many horses, whose figure awed him. Cataline quit packing in 1913, when the idea for a round-the-world, overland telegraph line fell through, and died in 1922. Then Byrnes took over. George Byrnes had a big ranch (Marty Allen's ranch now); only he wasn't a good organizer and when the trail closed down as a thoroughfare to the north for prospectors, he lost headway and finally shot himself. Late in life he had married the widow of a man who had disappeared on the trail.

At my friend from 1960, Jack Lee's, house, I ate a lunch of moose salami and fresh lettuce and spring onions, Frances's homemade bread, and root beer. Everybody's selling out to Californians here, they say—the Love families and the Lees, for 100,000 dollars or so—and building new houses on government ten-acre homesites that they apply for along the river at ten dollars an acre. They'll dig and roof the cellar first and live in that the first winter to avoid frost heaves. The Californians who move here to stay are good neighbors, but the speculators and summer parties are not. The world is filling up with Californians, just as California did.

I had phoned from Fort St. James, by chance, just before Jack and Frances set off on a prospecting trip. We're not going to Thutade Lake—we're going to a higher lake called Moosehorn, to stake lead and silver claims, instead. A windswept lake forms deeper ice because of having no cover of snow on it, and so is slower to clear. That's why the ice, he hears, is on Moosehorn still. Some of the Wooleys have gone bankrupt in the valley in the last year, Jack says, but some of the Simpsons have got rich. They found and sold a molybdenum claim for a quarter of a million dollars apiece. Finding themselves suddenly so rich, they went down to Vancouver to visit their daughter, but then they came back.

Jack says that Jack Lee Creek, a tributary of the Toodoggone River, in the Swannell Range, was named for him because he had so much trouble throwing a tree across it, in 1935, one time when he was with a survey crew and they needed to get across. He found this claim he wants to stake now, back in the 1940s, ten years later, when he was living close to the Caribou Hide hills. A loon is hollering, flying over us, as if it will rain tomorrow, he says. Says the wolves have got so bad up where we're going that in one fifteen-mile, wintering valley, the Moosehorn, one hundred caribou carcasses were left by them. He's only sixty-two, but rodeo-riding for years shook his insides up and aged him five to ten years, especially when a horse fell over onto him. Goes to a chiropractor for help, he says. It's raining again and thundering. The clouds build up above the existing mountains so they look twice as purple and twice as big. A puppy is on the floor, with pointy kit-fox ears, playing with its own penis like a child. The Allens, the Lees, and the two Love families are permanently beaming people. And there's work in the valley for everyone—crushing rock for the new roads, or in the sawmills or else in the woods, or building houses. Cable TV is coming to Hazelton, and they're having a banquet to pay for it. The Hazelton people want the Kispiox Valley people to contribute, but the Valley people, who are Indians, say, how about bringing us electricity first!

Jack is teaching his granddaughter to turn somersaults, as well as how a moose grunts. The Lees seem much happier as a family to me on this visit. The children have settled into their own family lives, since 1960, and Jack has adjusted to the process of aging. This evening he was out in the pasture making his first approach to a new colt. It's just a month old, and he kept his hands back by his waist and leaned forward towards it, face to face.

JUNE 19

Had home-cured bacon this morning (sugar, salt, saltpetre, and a good smoking), and cream from a bell jar on oatmeal. Jack changed the wick on the kerosene refrigerator. Then because the river is too high to fish, he napped on the rug, falling asleep immediately, with the baby napping right beside him. When he got up, he coughed for a couple of minutes to clear his lungs. I called Marty Allen on the ring-down phone and went over to see him, a mile down the road. He says that before the war, when he first went to work, in the thirties, he was earning ten dollars a week (twelve fifty if you did real well). This was in Fort Saskatchewan, and you wore fleece-lined long underwear that would freeze to your thighs from your sweat if you stopped. "Threshing" and "brushing" was the work. "You didn't need any blankets, just your lantern for warmth," you worked so hard, and the boss was so tough "he'd just as soon shoot you as look at you." Then Marty went to war in Europe, and saw one engagement where "our own tanks ran over our own wounded men" in an attack, they were moving so fast. They came home together—two thousand Canadians from Edmonton and the West—landed in New Jersey, and there were so many singing Italians ("Eye-talians") on the docks, Italian-Americans, that he thought for a moment he was back by the front. They marched across the George Washington Bridge, and then took the train to Boston, and to Toronto. At the border, Canadian girls in kilts met them, an awful pretty sight.

He bought his farm from George Byrnes, the fabled
Telegraph Trail packer, and a veteran of the Skagway 1898
gold rush, who finally shot himself, at seventy years old.
Peter Himadam packed for him, an Indian from Telegraph Creek. Peter used to take a big batch of George's
horses through to Caribou Hide, for wintering on the
Spatsizi Plateau, but one year they got a late start and
got snowed in on the Groundhog Pass, and Peter had to
shoot all fifty-six of them. Marty owns about one thousand acres, and has two thousand more that he's leased,
because the Americans have been tying up so much land
on the Kispiox River he felt he needed to protect himself.
Now, though, he's willing to sell out and retire on the pro-
ceeds. After the war, hay sold for fifty dollars a ton, but it's
down to thirty or forty dollars. Potatoes sold for ninety
dollars; now it's fifty dollars, after you count paying the
boys to wash them. Meat was, and still is only about forty-
five cents a pound. So now he's quit butchering. He sells
two hundred nine-month-old calves a year for 110 dollars
a head to a guy in Smithers, who fattens them for another
nine months.

He gives me coffee and cake, but tells some kids from
Hazelton over the phone that they can't come out because,
"If you've got other kids here, you can't get your own kids
to work. Or else they'll try to help but they'll pull everything but the weeds." Today he's been building a turnstile
gate that he can go through but the cattle can't. He says
that he shopped for Bruce Campbell, during Bruce's first

winter in the bush alone with a wife and child, "and gave him eleven cents change for a twenty-dollar bill." Campbell's total supplies (besides his own milk cow and garden) amounted to ten gallons of naphtha, ten gallons of coal oil, twenty pounds of rolled oats, one pound of coffee, one packet of pabulum, and four little tins of baby food. Then he didn't see him till March. A fellow in the valley (not Byrnes) shot himself, and they'd whispered that Bruce's father had done it, because it was thought that Bruce's father had come into the country originally from California because he had shot a Negro there and the police told him to clear out.

Marty's favourite stories are about his six-month winters, stationed at the Fifth Cabin on the Telegraph Trail, wherefrom he could go forty miles in a day, if he just stopped once in a while to wring the meltwater out of his socks. Just before he left, when the line and the trail were abandoned, he transplanted two hundred rhubarb plants from the roots of three plants that were growing there. He'd like to go back and see how they're doing. He packed a load of 120 pounds on his back one time, using a tumpline from his forehead—including three bear traps that he'd lifted from an Indian's cache. He says Gunanoot trapped for George Byrnes, during his three years on the loose in the bush, and finally came in to surrender with Byrnes. Gunanoot's son, Shelley, went to the war, and married a Scottish prostitute in Edinburgh. She used to pull Luke Fowler's braids, when she got drunk, and tell him to get a haircut. They arrested her for drunkenness with nothing on but her overshoes, and finally she died of cancer of the breast.

The cow at Jack Lee's hasn't calved yet, so Marty gave us some milk, and Frances gave Marty some carrots. Whether it's because I'm older now and less sexy, or whether it's that I'm married again and have nothing to prove, I'm not sexually hungry or preoccupied this summer. I just jerk off once a week into one of my socks, and that takes care of it, unlike in 1966.

JUNE 20

The Kispiox Tsimshian Indians, too, have a legend of a great flood. They say it was caused by an Indian who wasn't catching many fish. It was a bad season for everyone. After a whole day of trying, with only one salmon in hand, he held up the single fish towards the face of the mountain overhead that was their god, and cursed both god and mountain. Snow and rain fell for months on end, and the river rose till it almost covered the top of the mountain. Only two Indians still had survived by that time, a man and a woman. They built a raft, and they tied the raft to the peak of the mountain so that they didn't float away, and then they slept deeply, and when they woke up, the rains had let up. So they built a village on the other side of the river, when they started again.

Tommy Jack has been in the hospital a good deal lately. Besides him, the only old-timer left in town whom I remember from eight years ago is Arthur Hankin.

He uses a magnifying glass to read the notes that I pass him, and even then reads very slowly. Being deaf, he can't understand my stutter, and, of course, my head shakes particularly badly with anybody who is deaf. With a man in his nineties like this, who leans forward agitatedly to try and hear me, I get particularly blocked. Thus I imagine him having a heart attack while empathizing with me and straining to listen. He was born in Hazelton—almost the first white child—though they say if you ask him how old he is, he won't answer but will just tell you another story. His father came into the country for the Hudson's Bay Company a hundred years ago. His voice sounds young, clear, and resonant, though, and he lives in a rambling bare cabin with a linoleum floor and a pole roof, inside a cow pasture. The cow has an anchor attached to her chain. He used to walk up the Cariboo-Cassiar trail— as it was called before they put the telegraph line in—and worked for George Byrnes' great predecessor, Cataline, packing. Byrnes, he said, could put on a show of contortionist tricks, bending over backward and putting his head through his legs. He was a great hustler for money, but no organizer. He had carried the mail up the Skeena River to the gold mines, when making his start.

Hankin tells me a little bit more about Peter Himadam: that he was "peaceable," although Gunanoot's brother-in-law, and that he was finally found dead on a trail at the head of the Finlay, sitting up, but having simply played out. He'd been a fugitive with Gunanoot, but died before the surrender. Can't remember whether he had a family. What all these old fellows tell me first of all, even if they remember nothing else, is how the old-timers died. Bear Lake Charlie—a great hunter and traveller—still is alive, over one hundred—over in Topley. Then, over in Manson Creek, or up on the Omineca, were George Henny and Johnny Bryant, two gold commissioners, and lots of Chinese, working for the sixty years ending about 1930; and the three Condit brothers, who were Americans, in there at Tom Creek. And one of the luckiest men of all—Ezry Evans—at Blackjack Town Creek, who had a gold mine, but died in Hazelton. Never *was* poor.

Hankin worked on the Omineca River himself. Then there was also Jim Bouchet, who died when he was 103 years old. He drove a dogsled, and transported an accountant for the Hudson's Bay Company from each of the posts to another. One of the great dog handlers, he was always an early riser, needed no sleep, up at five every morning. But one morning he found he couldn't get up, and so he called all of the prospectors from all of the creeks around, and shook hands with them all, and told a few stories and jokes, gave his team away, and then died. He'd left Manitoba on foot with a flintlock and a fish net and walked all the way here, two thousand miles—pursued because of some arguments about his trading practices.

Hankin went up on the Finlay too, and walked to Telegraph Creek, and Hyland Post, and McConnell Creek, and
Caribou Hide, "just to see the country, to look the country
over," he says. He would have gone on to the Kechika, or
"Big Muddy," River, country; only it was too far. "You don't
mind walking out, but you don't like the walk back." Actually, he spent his whole life prospecting—many long summers alone. But he tells me not to use his name; doesn't
want "notoriety." He gets really disturbed, watching me
write. "Oh shit," he says. "You work me up too much. I
could tell you enough to fill up ten books, but I don't
want to." Now he claims to know nothing at all, and not
to have been much of a prospector himself anyway—it's
only an accident that he is the one who has survived for so
long. He's a tall, rangy, deeply stooped man with a likable,
bespectacled, long, benign face. Can't seem to tell me anything about people, though—only the facts, what they did,
where they lived—even when he's cooperating. Though he
was a man of many hallucinations when he was all alone,
and an imaginative storyteller when he was with friends,
he never seems to think in terms of personality, only of
jobs, territories, and facts. Since he's stopped enjoying our
talk, I feel his helplessness, with me in the kitchen stub-
bornly pressing another question on the heels of the last,
and him so old. I feel I'm picking on him, so I get up to
leave. As I do, however, I ask if I can come back, and he says
yes. I ask if he'll tell me more stories if I do. Yes, he says.

I spent part of the evening hearing some of Hankin's favourites from other people (which was a sneaky thing to do)—like about the angel's feather. He was climbing a mountain one summer, after being out for the winter, too. He was a little bit "bushy," as they call it, in his head, and he saw what looked like an angel's feather lying on the trail. He tried to pick the thing up, but it kept blowing ahead. He followed, and followed, and finally it blew right into the mouth of a cave. And there was Moses sitting there. He said, "Hi, Moses." And Moses said, "Hi, Art..." Another year he came into some distant country where several miners had wintered, and it had been so cold that their words had froze in the air. He got there during the month of May, when the warm thaw came, so he could hear the words as they thawed out. These told him how cold it had been. It was so cold the smoke from the chimney had frozen into a pillar towering in the air, and they'd chopped that down and sawed it up and built a house out of the blocks, a real "smokehouse..." They were shooting at grouse, and one guy was so good he could shoot a grouse's head off—nothing more—so as not to hurt the meat. But another guy, he could shoot and slit its throat with the bullet, in order to save even the head for soup.

Hankin mostly walked, but he was a sturdy packer, people say: Up in the middle of the night and chasing two miles in his long johns and hat and boots, if the horses had started to head for home. Crossing the Sustut River once, he was on a horse that somehow or other didn't know how to swim. They'd put him on her because he could. But the horse went under, all right, and not only under, but did a complete belly-roll—the gasping nostrils upside down were the only part of her that showed. She came up like a fearful hippo, and old Arthur slid off. Swim or not, if there hadn't been an old Indian fishing slough by the ford for them to float into, he might have drowned. There were so many black flies in that north country you needed to hold your breath to keep from breathing them in. The Indians had left an old woman to die in a cabin on Black-water Creek, as was their wont in the winter, when they moved through. But that spring she was still alive some-how; she'd had enough wood to keep a fire going, plus cornmeal, and her dog had stayed behind. But they left her again the next fall, and that year the old girl did die.

I wanted this to be an introspective journal, and a rather introspective summer, too, what with my second marriage, and my first child on the way, and my father twelve months dead. But so many stories, people, and facts keep crowding me that I'm simply too busy paying attention and writing them down to consider much of anything else. I'd have to lose interest in all of this jump and life and adventure. Yet if I'd lost interest, I wouldn't have come in the first place. I'm living in the utmost inti-macy with this Lee family, working (and reading bear books) while they fidget at life, in the manifold tensions and pleasures it holds. As busy or bustly as all of us are, the wonder is not that we sleep away one-third of our lives but that we don't have to sleep more.

And the prospecting bug has hit this north country again. What with the ubiquitous bush pilots and planes, and the boom in ground transportation, the floods of investment money from Vancouver or the East pouring in, and the rise in the price of metals, everybody who's ever been out in the bush remembers some outcropping or other he once saw, or that a Caribou Hider or Bear Laker once led him to, and has flown back recently and staked it. Tomorrow Jack and Frances, his endearing wife (energetic, affectionate, efficient), are taking me out to do just that—revisit his youth, hopes, and memories. My hair has grown nice and long to keep out the cold and, since I haven't caught the flu bug which has been going around the Lee family, it should be a marvellous week, though on the whole a wet and cold June. New snow on the mountains every morning.

A boy and a girl walk towards a boy sitting alone in a field in the chill of the evening. "You want us to teach you how to kiss?" they call to him. He shakes his head. "You better learn it from me," she adds, "because it wouldn't look very good if you learned it from him." I'm reading *Oliver Twist*, which reminds me of my three years on the Lower East Side, when I saw a number of ragged tiny kids nabbed for theft, whimpering in the grip of a shopkeeper—maybe their mother there too in tears—whimpering to be let go before the cops arrived, and all that bazaar going on around them.

How strange these women from the bush look when they have lipstick on. It's just dabbed on them like a spot of red.

JUNE 21

Lee mimics people unexpectedly, like my father did. He has quite a similar accent, really, and the same unexpected directness, from out of the quiet manner. His methodical competence at what he's good at is rather like Dad's thinking competence, too.

The planes on the little lake at Smithers look bug-little, but they take off with a bold prolonged roar, like a trombone's blare. Finally it's our turn; and Lee's sipping whisky to quiet his nerves (Seagram's Special Old—or "ground-softener," as the prospectors call it); and, with a Love family man along, we jalopy into the air: the lake in the Bulkley Valley brown but sparkling underneath us. I have the usual nervous sore throat and flu stomach this morning, but forget them, looking down at the thousand shades of green, and the pale green gullies. The plane is a Beaver, and the pilot a bluff blond named Bill Harrison, of Omineca Airlines. He charges seventy-two cents a mile, and my share is about two hundred of them. We climb east into an ore-red pass, cutting in close to save gas. There are brilliant snow splatters across the rock, then tiny, aquamarine-coloured creeks that braid through the flats. Snow speckles the conifer forest. We cross an irregular burn, our lives filled with the engine's roar, and cross some mountains—Blunt, Netalzul and Thoen— each striped like a zebra with snow; and see Babine Lake, almost as long as a river. We fly through several attenuated clouds, bar-like, with black glimmering lakes chaining below in a limitless forest.

The Babine River is brown and seems scaled, lizarding along. Swaying in a silly-dilly fashion, we cross over Mount Lovell and Frypan Peak, not too high, but a long snowy line of concise cusps. On the other side is a large flat valley with green shallow rivers around Takla Lake, which is large and amoeba-shaped, fed by the Driftwood Valley, still larger. Then Bear Lake, which consists of long twists and one loop. Then some green pocket lakes and a low cloud front; a large belt of snowy highlands, and another big churning river, the Omineca, with a burn on one side and a forest on the other. Now there's a regular wilderness of mountains everywhere, McConachie and Oakes and Gil and Hewett, with the steep irregular valleys between; the grey-green Sustut River, and a lush rug of forest. Then an absolute ocean of mountains strewn and feathered with snow, Kubicek, and Stalk Peak, and Red Crag, which the pontoon below me seems to move sedately across. These include the lovely, pearly Brothers Peaks, dusted with snow. Then a brown muskeg valley, practically treeless, Brothers Lake, Jellico Creek, Chapelle Creek, and brilliant snow on the next ridge, which is Lawyers Pass. Then two expansive green valleys which meet like a carpenter's rule. The Sturdee River, the Firesteel River were giant long wiggles of water in gently sloped valleys which were forested heavily except for a burn at one end. We've left the Skeena Mountains and the Tatlatui Range for the Samuel Black Range, and Bill, the pilot, names the lakes jokingly to Jack, who helped to survey this stretch of wilderness as a young man in 1935—then got lost trying to come back here again in 1948. And Bill says teasingly, "There's a dandy wolf crop—seen lots of cubs."

We cross over a wilderness of kettle holes near Pan Creek and Black Lake, another burn, and a snow-spotted forest. Saunders Creek is high and an ashy grey except where it's marked with curly rapids. Then comes a mass of brown, burned-over, eroded mountains, Mount Graves, Mount Estabrooke, Mount Gordonia, Mount Catherine, dozens of them, uncountable, it seems—no straight valleys—Mount Hartley, The MacGregors, the land slashed as if by psychic scars. We slant over a murderous-looking pass at Toodoggone Peak and bank steeply down, yawing, the mountains sunless and black, the choppy land angling crazily underneath us.

By a little lake is a neat mining camp of even white tents. Each has a wooden floor built up on logs, when we get inside. The cook's is postered with twenty pin-ups, lusciously nude ("quite a kennel," says Bill), but there are topographic maps up, too—and slabs of bread on the shelf, just out of the oven, and cheesecloth laid over steaks. We get these, and tomatoes and cucumbers, served. It's the Cordilleran Exploration Company (a subsidiary of US Steel) base camp, from which two helicopters shuttle prospecting crews out and about. There are red barrels everywhere full of airplane fuel. This camp is a few hundred feet below timberline. The cindery, blocky mountaintops crowd close around, streaked with snow. Toodoggone Lake is only about a mile long but simmers with shadow and shine in the wind, and Jack Lee Creek flows into the Toodoggone River nearby.

Even the refrigerator is plastered with the showy pin-ups, brought by the cook from Ottawa. People have signed their names across different girls' hips to indicate who belongs to whom. Leo, the cook, seems very womanly (though is probably a lady's man), and it's like here he works surrounded by his twenty girlfriends. He told us about his adventures at the end of the lake with a lady moose. And there was a lady beaver, too, that slapped its tail on the water and got him wet. The pilot, Bill, shot ninety-eight wolves and 160 coyotes, he claims, one winter, with a rifleman—for the bounty and to sell the fur—making a living, but finally he dissolved his wolf-hunting partnership, when the other guy blamed a missed wolf on *his* flying and he blamed it on *his* shooting. There are more moose and caribou then ever before, and also more wolves than any time since World War II.

Jack Lee tells the story of his misbegotten trip here in 1948, when the horses got "mountain fever" (altitude sickness), and were cutting their hocks in the crusty snow: this being only during late August. Lee also once paddled and poled into this country from the Finlay on a two-log raft. He could have walked easier, but he wanted to fish, and the Toodoggone River is so high and curvy and close to its source that it mostly purls. The Toodoggone is where a McLair that Jack knew, and McLair's partner, also from Hazelton, prospected for nearly ten years, till one winter, in the early 1930s, they both just disappeared. George Byrnes followed their nightly camps back towards the Finlay and decided that they'd probably gone through the ice. Their old hut is across the lake from us, with a hole now where its door was. Jack says you can find a few grains of gold in their old sluice boxes, that have softened and rotted.

A helicopter is a queer black assemblage of equipment, bubble-topped—a rearview mirror is strapped on one of the struts—with the vicious, whipping, whacking noise of the blade overhead. Continuing on to his claim at Moosehorn Lake, we strap our duffels onto the slings. It's a million-dollar ride. Seventy miles per hour, and the country laid out sliding by. Open, hammocky valleys with balsam and spruce and pothole ponds. Saw four moose on Mulvaney Creek, and a caribou; also a dark-coloured bear up on a slide near Contact Peak swinging his cautious nose. I looked down and saw a caribou's antlers below on the ground. Each creek valley—Midas Lake, Upper Belle Lake, Hiamadam Creek—individually seemed to belong to us, and the mountains had been named by geologists, because no other white men had bothered. Oxide Peak, Tuff Peak, Breccia Peak.

Our camp is three hundred feet below timberline, sheltered by two low spruce. Still air; occasional rain; temperature probably forty. We have a silk tent with a fly stretched in front for additional shelter, and a cooking fire in front of the fly. The Lees' anticipation, excitement and talk about being in God's Country is effervescent. Had Frances's canned moosemeat for supper, and we sit in a yoga position to keep our butts off the wet ground. Then Jack sits on the pan of a moose antler he's found, which looks like a big willow leaf. The stream, Tseehee Creek, shimmies by, so lifelike that it seems like more wildlife. We lay our sleeping bags on balsam branches for a mattress. The balsam trees have trunks blue with lichen. Three fluttery caribou came capering almost into camp while we were eating. Their coats looked as white as the stream, and they were pretending to browse, but really they were there to watch us. I slept in a tent with Wally Love, who got a heavy pistol out, what with the three men in Jasper

Park mauled by a grizzly bear just before I got there, and Wally's own close call with a grizzly last year. I'm glad he has it—my feelings about the assassinations of the Kennedys and Martin Luther King quite aside.

Stories from Lee: The Tahltan Caribou Hiders out beating pots and hollering, when they saw a grizzly on the mountainside. And a mining camp cook putting his hat over the stovepipe to trap a hatful of heat in the winter, then putting his hat on and going out and giving his friends a dose of it. Jack himself had fried his eggs on the blade of his shovel, so as not to have to bring a pan— eggs so old that "they crowed when they hit the metal." Cooked his breakfast-fish on the end of a string, which he would spin with his fork over the fire ("spun-cooked"). His wife Frances had felt she had to go to church every week—or at least a couple of times during the summer— so she hadn't come with him. But now she's the life of our party—plump, merciful, muscular, full of laughter.

Oh, this abrupt, air age! We are under Claw Mountain.

JUNE 22

Buckwheat hotcakes, bacon, and eggs for breakfast. In a pool not far from here in Moosehorn Creek, Jack says you can count the Dolly Varden before you even start fishing for them, and they all go for the hook as it hits the clear water. When he walked the Telegraph Trail with Maunkton, the surveyor, one winter, they saw a moose at the Second Cabin, in a side river, which had thrashed a sixty-foot space free of ice for itself. They let that one go, because it was early in the day, and they already had full packs on their backs, but then they didn't see another moose until they got all the way clear to the Little Klappan River, maybe a hundred miles. However, they shot up to twenty-five ptarmigan a day, in order to feed themselves and the sled dogs. One dog had swallowed its daily ptarmigan whole, and choked, and Jack broke a gun stock on him. Didn't see caribou either—though the caribou, when he ruts, has a lovely white cape that you want. At the Klappan, they met a young man who was attempting to ski from Fairbanks to Chicago, but who had had to abandon his skis and go on snowshoes.

With me in my city cap, and socks on my hands to serve for gloves, we went out "prospecting." Some prospectors who have been out all summer—you can still see the price written on the shovel, Jack says. They may have done their "assessment" work mostly with one single dynamite charge. A claim is fifty-one acres, and to register it costs thirty dollars, plus the miner's licence is five dollars; and the yearly assessment work is supposed to amount to one hundred dollars worth, minimum. Jack and his partners have a total of six claims, and we're here, quite simply, because thirty-three years ago Jack was working through these valleys of the Metsantan Range as part of a survey crew, at four dollars a day, and saw, about quitting time, from where they were camped in the timber, a sort of white stain on the mountainside above him—almost like a stripe that somebody might have painted with lime dust. He'd climbed up there secretly when he had a chance and dug two feet down with his shovel, finding a lead, silver, zinc, or galena vein. It was "native lead" that you could peel with the blade of your knife, in any case, he thought, and with a double ore like that (or tungsten-gold, for instance), the company which works the mine will eventually hope to pay the expenses of the operation out of one of the metals produced, while the other can give you your profit. But he'd covered his discovery over then, carefully—even to replacing the tussocks of turf—because in those days, before you started to think about a mining company paying you a bundle of money for your claim, you were trying to prevent them or somebody else from beating you out of it. Finally, last year, chartering a plane, and running around for six hours, building cairns (or "witness posts"), he did the proper staking, to the best of his recollection. We're here now to try to find the lead again and see if his memory was right, after thirty-some years.

The shoulder of Mount McNamara has "got steeper," he says, because one mile is like ten miles was to him then. No white stain shows, as we climb, and he talks about needing X-ray eyes—"Superman eyes." There's a thick overburden of soil and turf even above timberline, which is furred with ground scrub, ground balsam, or junipers. We dig down to the frost line several different times, and chip below that with a miner's pick. The ground is spongy above, and soft; the snows maybe two-thirds off. Where it isn't gone, the groundhogs above and below us lope across like fleas on a white bedsheet to the next patch of grass. There are a good many groundhog holes, and plenty of excavations that the bears have made after them—sometimes whole trenches, or big, virile-looking, military foxholes they've dug. The grizzlies had also knocked over an interloper's stone cairn this spring, which he seemed to have built not very much better than a bear would have done. We saw one old set of bear tracks, melted so that they looked larger than its feet really were. On the way out, Jack got a cock ptarmigan with his .22 pistol. It hadn't flown, and it closed its eyes and died. During the summer, the only white feathering you see on them is when they fly, but now, so early, he was mottled and grousey, as well as white, with long pretty claws, a seed-eater's beak, and red eyebrows, handsome and neat. Except for cutting off his head and feet, Wally cleaned him just using his hands; stripped and gutted him.

Again like my dad, Jack can make an occasional bit of fun of himself, but can't accept any hint of outside criticism. It's been a discouraging day for him: no trace of the lead on his claim—so he wonders how much he's forgotten in thirty-three years—and a tremendous heaviness in his legs, the mark of aging. And he took several shots to hit the ptarmigan, though it stood still for him. Then he shot at the head of a buttercup four or five times, to make up for that, and missed. In the evening he took a walk down the valley by himself to buck up his spirits. The valley spreads out like a miniature plain, except that it's sopping and tangled with arctic birch. The water hasn't anywhere to run, so it runs everywhere, and meets Dedeeya Creek, also quite wet. One time he saw a mysterious serpent, he says, in Chukachida Lake. It bobbed and undulated. So he was mystified, until he recognized that it was really a family of otters, who were "holding onto each other's tails" as they swam along. It *is* nice, anyway, for him to have a younger man here taking down practically his every word.

JUNE 23

I talk to my Marion whenever I'm alone for a few minutes. In fact, last night I dreamed that an old acquaintance of mine was trying to seduce me, and after a great deal of vacillating, I manfully refused. Sleeping on a bed of balsam boughs, with foam rubber on top of that, and then the sleeping bag, isn't exactly tough! The caribou winter down by Metsantan Lake, under Alberts Hump, in the Stikine Valley, but the moose winter right in around here, eating the knickinick and ground balsam. In the summer they eat fireweed, willow, and red osier.

I spent today by myself, walking up and partly around a spur of Claw Mountain—nothing too strenuous. It was the first sunny day in a week. I took hotcake sandwiches, and also an axe, for the idea that I was protected, and spent a lay-about day, mostly sitting by brooks, looking into the pools, at the moss and the bright-coloured rocks on the bottom. There is practically any noise you want to hear embedded in the noise a brook makes—from a thin, wavering scream to a jolly, tuba-voiced conversationalist. I saw lots of moose and caribou sign but started up nothing except ptarmigan—that shallow, quarrelsome cackle they have—eating willow buds. The trees age fast in this brutal climate, and don't grow very high, and there are frequent breaks in the forest—mossy, grassy, or lichenous clear-ings, which link up with one another and are well marked by the caribou as feeding grounds. It's an open country. All around are unnamed, unnumbered little mountains speckled with snow, enclosing side valleys, too many to explore even if you had the whole summer. The animals have moved out (it's easy to see why so many travellers on these trails have gone without fresh meat for weeks), and, since the helicopter dropped us, there's been no sign of another human being, either.

One of the problems I'm trying to resolve this summer is where to live. Nobody seems to want to live anywhere now. The suburbanites wish they were living in town and the city people wish that they had a country home. Of course the farmer, too, wants to get off his farm. So what we generally choose—those few of us who are positioned by our profession to choose—is enclave-living: twenty cheap acres somewhere, and exotic getaway trips occasionally, with the recognition that a good part of the year may be spent in a place we'd really not prefer.

It's such an anachronism in this contemporary world to worry about grizzly bears, yet here I am, taking a Contac pill with its "thousand tiny time capsules" for a cold, and worrying about meeting a bear today or tomorrow on my walks, though no more strange than walking the streets in fear of a beating, as we do in New York. I'm glad I wrote *Notes from the Century Before* when I did. I still love the sound of the cataract outside the tent, but have less patience than in 1966. I was in the "workhouse" before supper with *Oliver Twist,* while Jack was practising with his pistol, a weird juxtaposition. I'm not as receptive now, and couldn't have written that same book this year.

Supper was steaks from a yearling Smithers moose (tastes like horse), and rice boiled three-quarters of an hour, and dried apples, also boiled. Lee says Relief during the Hungry Thirties was six dollars per week per head. He just stumbled on that survey job on the Finlay while he was prospecting through on his own. After supper, he went out and sat on a knoll overlooking the valley to wait for game. I strolled out too, and stayed a while longer, my heart bleeding for all my past failures in marriage and love.

They clipped some promising silver-ore fragments today out of a bed on Deer Creek. Wally was busy scratching information on the metal claim tags which they will put out tomorrow. I'm stuttering badly, as I generally do with non-bookish people, unfortunately. So I don't say much, and let lots of misinformation go past unchallenged: of which nothing is more galling. The subjects range from the origins of granite, to wolves and snakes, to local geography. Seven caribou, including two well-antlered bucks, were seen today by the others.

JUNE 24

So here I am, right where I wanted to be, in the midst of the central experience of this summer, which I've looked forward to. We're approximately a two-hundred-mile walk from the nearest road. We're really alone—almost as alone as it's physically possible to be, on this earth nowadays—and is it so different? Of course it's not as savagely lonely as the city can be, because if you're lonely in the city there's no hope. For me it's a period of gassing up. I have to gas up on solitude, just as I do on company at other times. But, actually, when you come right down to it, could I do just as well if I were only ten miles from the nearest road, instead of two hundred?

When I was nineteen and took care of three or four tigers for Ringling Bros. and Barnum & Bailey, I was fearless during the day, but dreamt horrendously about them at night. Here it's the opposite. My dreams are placid, but I walk in the woods in considerable trepidation. It's that the grizzly, in what we know about him, is so manlike. As everyone says, "You can come on him everywhere."

A "Chinaman" in Hazelton named Jack Lee used to receive Lee's land tax bill in the mail, and pay it, and Lee would receive *his* Indian girlfriends' letters. Sometimes he cooked bird's nest soup, and when he cooked rice, he knew when to take it off the fire simply by pulling a handful of steam towards him and smelling it.

The old bone-rattler, the wolf, pulls a caribou's hind skin forward and the front skin back.

Horse parasites are found in certain hollow-stemmed grasses.

Some of the old prospectors liked to smoke up their clothes before they came into town, so they'd smell less stinky. In other words, they would run chimney smoke through their sleeves.

Oliver Twist has that elemental storytelling force, but Dickens's villains are blacker than the villains I've known, and his heroes of course are whiter. Sometimes one wishes they weren't caricatures.

JUNE 25

A day off. A rainy day. I daydream a little about sex—a kinky slave merchant—and the Lees and Wally Love talk about money, land deals, etc. British Columbia is booming.

Land, in fact, is more expensive than in Vermont, and wages are up to four dollars an hour. House lots in town cost three or four thousand and the house itself an additional eighteen thousand. Everybody is selling their old place and buying a new one. Vermont, at a hundred dollars an acre and a house for five thousand, seems more like the place for me to live, because even the incomparable emptiness here is being opened up fast.

The eggs are a bit strong today. You cook eggs hard so that you don't have to wash the plate much. You cut bacon off the slab and use the outer skin for soup. A lot of chopping today, building up the fire. It rained so hard the fry pan half filled up with water before the dinner was done. "Is that right?" says Jack a lot, and ends many of his comments with "anyway"—a qualifier. Some of the old prospectors would cook in their gold pans and eat off their shovels. Others took only a fry pan, a knife, and a cup as extra implements—the fry pan for boiling coffee water, too. Coffee goes right to the bladder like beer, and we sit in camp watching the creek wink and glimmer at the head of the draw. White mountains through the trees in two directions, looking very close, and a wind that blows right from the snow.

Frances is invariably energetic and enthusiastic, cheerful and kind. Always, out on the hikes, her plumpness slows her down, but never impedes her for long. She's always with Jack, even out in the sharp rain that punctuated the afternoon, good-humouredly taking his teasing and the rigorously hidebound speeches he makes about the virtues of caribou meat, the adulteration of modern life, and so on. He walks with such a short man's ground-covering lunge that it looks as if he's just walked twenty miles, whether it's one or whether it's actually twenty. Wally Love is in his mid-forties but looks ten years younger than that. A mild man, always with the seeds of a smile on his face, he prefers photographing game to shooting it. Slow to action too, Lee is a wry-faced, tough old socialist, who wears heavy tweed wool pants, and "braces," and has raised many neighboring boys. He says that the bleach in white sugar or white rice will eat your insides out and do away with your teeth. Likewise the "tenderizer" which he says is injected into store meat.

In this northern country, as high as we are, the trees are mostly balsam. The spruce and Jack pine don't go above four thousand feet, and the big birches not above two thousand. Wolverines, wolves, and bears are the predators. Wolverines travel tirelessly at a lope, with tail low. Every once in a while one will jump completely around with its head facing you, but the tail up like a skunk's. Ptarmigan eat the buds of the arctic plants. The whole bird is as red as beef liver when skinned, and brown as beef liver after it's cooked. It's not as good as they say—not as good as the willow grouse—but I found it good: quietly, stewingly stringy and gamey. Of course I had pictures of the living bird in my head, in its ignorant, complex, parti-coloured plumage.

Arthur Hankin talked of the Fountain of Youth that he found somewhere way out in the bush, and of a sea serpent in Babine Lake which loomed above the water sixty feet. "You mean six feet?" I asked. "Six feet between the eyes," he said.

There are so many incomplete characters in Dickens, and yet like an artist who knows how to use a couple of lines, he does get them fixed, he gets them *down*. It's such a squally and mist-bound day that when I'm not reading *Oliver Twist* I'm thinking of gruesome city scenes the book reminds me of. I remember in Boston, in the West End, which is now entirely demolished, seeing a man come round a corner carrying a cane and following a staggering or tottering fellow, whom he was whipping with regular blows as they walked, and my witnessing all of it made no interruption, since I was a mere boy. He kept whacking him all the time, and finally into and up the steep stairwell of a tenement house.

In San Francisco I knew a girl who was in her mid-twenties and who had two children and a sailor boyfriend. She'd hang a towel in her window whenever she wanted him to stop by. She had been whipped with a hose from an automobile engine as a girl, and often, so that she raised no objection when he whipped her little girl, who was three or four. This he did so frequently and strenuously as to change the girl's character in a matter of months. They shuttled her in and out of a foster home, besides, where the husky matron assured us she taught the children to do their duty as regards the toilet, but let no affectionate attachments form.

I remember, again, on the Lower East Side, two parents dragging a child along, her feet lifted clear off the sidewalk, while she pleaded pathetically not to be beaten. Everything and everybody along the street came to a standstill at the clear pathos in that voice—and people began to follow in order to put a stop to the crime. It was obvious she was beaten as often as she was fed. But we didn't put a stop to it because once the lout of a father and red-faced mother, dragging the child between them, gained their own building, then none of us followed, it being an inviolate rule that a man's house is his castle—dungeon and all.

JUNE 26

To the stream's metallic clatter and the sunlight through the tent, with tree branches traced on it: that's how we all wake up. We lie abed till eight. People in the bush get lots and lots of sleep, and being rednecks usually, don't use toothbrushes or napkins. When one of the early white babies was born in the Kispiox Valley, they took the mother to the barn and made a couch of hay for her, so that the other kids wouldn't hear her scream, and they brought in the sled dogs and other animals and packed them in around close to help keep her warm.

Take a cake of soap into the bush for washing yourself and for the dishes, and a pot with a loop over the top for hanging on a crosspiece over the fire, and a beaver hat that you could also use for a bucket. A mare gave birth to a colt in a cold creek, and when they found it, the foal looked dead, so they poured rum down its throat and soaked it in a washtub of warm water until life began coming back.

The suddenness with which strangers used to come into camp—their momentum and silent tread. Aside from the Sustut River, where Wally almost drowned, their most dangerous crossing on one survey was the Babine, which goes through a canyon sixty feet deep. There was a shaky wooden Indian suspension bridge, which they took the horses across one at a time, and very slowly. If they'd let the horses hurry across, they would have broken through. With hats steaming from an all-day rain, they'd sit by the fire at night, cutting slivers of orange cheese and eating these off the knife. Different horses swim differently, one with its whole body thrust a foot out of the water, and one with just its eyes and nostrils showing.

They'd scrounged old cigarette butts from behind a trapper's stove in an abandoned cabin. Macaroni put in cold water, by a bad cook, goes to glue, and they found some in old pots. Eating sandhill cranes in the fall; and geese and tundra swans were good, too, just before the first snowfall, after they'd been down from the north fattening a while, and when the rutting caribou were fighting the trees. There was the moose they saw trying to escape uphill from a pond in midwinter with a crust on the snow, breaking through, and lying there exhausted and helpless at last, when they were chasing it on snowshoes. And the trouble the long nose and lip and dewlap of a moose gives when you're skinning it. They'd watched two Indians going up the fissures of a cliff like two red squirrels; and Jack was smoking the chewing tobacco—greasy and sweet—with which he had hoped to break his smoking habit. On the Finlay River they kept "water-glass eggs," because there was a substance you put into water—you filled a ten-gallon can and put in the eggs—that forms a preserving glaze on the surface of the eggs. Of course you had assorted eggs, assorted colours and flavours, brown, white, sour and sweet. You needed them all for your health. The guys who lived on nothing but beans and bannock got scurvy from eating the starch, Jack says. "Your blood gets so thick it won't flow. You have to take vinegar or spruce tea to thin it." This one guy had used to weigh 180 pounds, but he'd shrivelled to ninety from constant diarrhea. His gums and his skin turned black from scurvy. Finally he couldn't even lift his hands. They killed him a moose and fed him some of that, till he was strong enough to be packed out on a sled and put on a boat. His fingers and toes had fallen off.

Joe Hamburger ("Hamburger Joe") had left Fort Gra-hame, on the Finlay, with Jack for a five-mile walk to a mountaintop across the river, where some caribou were wintering. He was "as tough as whalebone," but he got one foot wet in the overflow on the ice and he wouldn't go back to change, or complain; only stopped to kick his boot against a tree to help restore the circulation occasionally. So his foot froze on the hunt, and gradually the tip joints of all the toes fell off; then the flesh from the second joints too. He went around with the ends of his shoe and sock cut off, and you'd hear the toe bones click on the floor. The little-toe bone fell off by itself, and finally one day when the first boat arrived in the spring, and he was running to meet it, he stubbed the big-toe remnant and stopped and ripped off what was left of it as well. He'd been a loner, a busher, also in civilian life.

Jack seems to admire suffering for the sake of the suffering, and ignorance for its setting. His standard is stoicism. You could pooh-pooh all of this, say Joe Hamburger gave himself up to the ethic right away, almost wanted to get his toes frozen off to prove to himself he could stand it, but I tend not to, believing I'm witnessing how the continent was settled. And Jack wants competition, wants to shoulder as heavy a pack as possible, and wants a boy to exhort, so since he hasn't got one of those at the moment, he uses his wife for that office. At breakfast, they told me—as so many people do, hearing me stutter and making a connection—about the cripples they get in the bush when guiding customers—the man who came out with throat cancer, three months to live, and the severe asthmatic who couldn't walk fifty feet in a hurry.

We walked up the valley through the hump-brush with packs to above Moosehorn Lake—rather a commonplace name for a lake which lies near the very head of the Finlay-Peace-Mackenzie River, Arctic Ocean watershed. We looked up at the passes and saddles along the way, where you'd probably find goats' wool on the ground, and on the other side, Pacific Ocean streams. The hills have turned June-green in just the five days we've been here. There are hogbacks along the sides of the upper valley, with meadows between them. We saw a few shelterless lemmings darting, and a large wolf's fresh track near an old denning area that Jack remembers. Jack has a jaw like Popeye the Sailorman. In the creek, you take off your shoes and wade barefoot, or else tie your pant legs tightly to your boots so your boots don't fill. Why is it we get such deep satisfaction from the struggle and discomfort of lugging a heavy pack on long hikes—and not only people like Lee, whose lifelong vocation it justifies, but also people like me? Surely it's not simply the stoic and manly tradition. Isn't it our instinct for self-preservation, our gladness to feel that we still can *go,* still survive a trip, carrying our necessities along with us? But it's gotten confusing for people like Jack, when there are so many new ways of being a man; the old criteria have been eclipsed.

I remember the frantic Greeks, chased by the Syracusans, who fled and were caught at the river in the Sicilian desert, drinking thirstily, and how they were butchered or spared according to how they drank. I've tried drinking from these creeks in the manner of the Greeks who were butchered, and also like the Greeks who were spared, and I prefer the way of the ones who were butchered. It's true that a noble-spirited man wouldn't sprawl on his stomach to suck the water, but if you sacrifice your nobility, you can see right into the pools, see the pebbles and moss. (I've been to Greece and to Syracuse.)

Then when I took off my pack, my shoulders felt so airy and light that balloons might have been attached to them; I could hardly walk straight. The lake lies just at timberline. The trees are my own height and the ground rolls in primitive humps, as though it has not existed here long enough to have formed a level surface. The slab-cut, rudimentary mountains only go up a thousand feet more, with green mossy sides or grey rock-facing, and snow wherever the snow could catch in a cleft. There are ground squirrels, marten tracks hunting the squirrels, and a pair of beautifully grizzled-grey whistlers, as alert as badgers, who looked in fighting trim. The female crouched in front of the male, and they looked to be thriving, indeed. Six swallows swarmed in the air, sharp-winged, swinging like jets. We found a snipe's nest with eggs in the grass, and I found a tiny nest in a bush next to my head with three tiny soundless babies in it, reaching for food. Both parents put on a crippled show.

Here we are at the head of this wild river system and there are five full fifty-five-gallon gasoline cans on the bank, left over from float-plane and helicopter camps.

At the very head of the valley is a clear pass which you couldn't see through till you got nearly to the top—only saw sky. Then, climbing up, you saw another chunky peak straight-on, with mammoth Japanese script scrawled on it in the snow. I scrambled into a stubby tree on a height and saw down a U-walled, precipitous, black-rock declivity—Straight Pass Creek—to the valley of the Chukachida, finally, and Pacific-flowing water. The peak at first had looked only moderate in height, and "open-armed." Then, closer, it seemed much larger in its dimensions, complicated in its spurs and coils and snowed-in pockets, and clouds surrounded and veiled it: McNamara.

I walked warily, but nowhere was there bear sign. Numbers of caribou and moose had previously passed through, but the point about this country is its emptiness. Through these huge wintery valleys, dominated by snowfall, the game, like ourselves, only traverses. The ground is as bumpy and mossed-over as though the week of Creation were just over. Most of the caribou lichen, white, green, and speckled with blue, never gets eaten, and the bunch grass quietly cures itself in the sun.

We had rice and raisins for supper, with milk and sugar on top. At timberline, the firewood is as twisted as piled antlers, and afterward Lee was out breaking rocks from the vales and the slides, the "float" that tells what rocks lie higher up—the "drift," the "overburden." He looks carefully backward every so often as he goes, in order not

to get lost. The ignorance of prospectors about rocks and
geology, however, is sad to see. They say they want a "very
old" rock, a "very crushed," a "very heated" rock for minerals, and then they see a conglomerate and think that's
just the thing. But Jack, of course, isn't lazy. For most of
them, people say, "you couldn't follow that prospector by
his trail of broken rock," because he didn't break many.
But Jack goes out to knock the mountain apart, looking
for lead, to crack it good, burping loudly when he's tired,
and seeming to profit and renew himself by his burps. I'm
rather stuffed-up sick of all his opinionated pronounce-
ments, the talk about whose area is whose, whose area
is bigger, the "plague of wolves," and where to mine, the
relish with which he tells grisly stories of kills, poisonings
and mishaps. He coughs like a death's head and his face
is as drawn as an old consumptive's. Maybe my reactions
are not without prejudice. Maybe the certain resemblance
to my own father is triggering ulterior annoyances in me.

JUNE 27

Today is all storms and wind. Hail hit our tents during the
night and lots of rain, and there was snow only a little bit
higher. I woke up hearing coughing and realized it was me.
I laid my coat over my head with a Coricidin dissolving on
my tongue, until it put me to sleep. Sometimes they don't
have any summer here at all. Winter slacks off and leads
into the next winter. Though my cough's like the bark of

a fox, I took my morning shit on a high point to have time to look about. There were red-headed, grey, finch-sized birds active and singing—birds are active anywhere any time, they're so hot-blooded. I walked up another pass towards the Chukachida and the drainage of the Stikine, with clear, snow-water pools in every depression, clean, crisp-looking and crusted with ice on the edges, like miniature cirques or hanging glaciers. The trees were sparsely clustered; the ground in between a rough tundra. Some of the snow was stained red from myriad moss spores. There was a loud waterfall off a nearby mountain, and some bear diggings dating to last fall. Yet here you are at the top and centre of the world, at the headwaters of two great drainages, and where it isn't tundra, it's mud. You sink in every few steps, but the country is much more open-looking than lower down. The creek going towards the Stikine almost immediately grows healthy and big, winding down its pass through increasingly sturdy, thick timber towards a blue and white world standing precipitously on end. Yet a valley barren so far of whistlers.

Jarringly, my companion on occasion during these latter unsettling couple of days—who puts me to sleep at night and goes with me sometimes on hikes—is a blind slave girl. Or else the relationship is reversed and masochistically I "belong" to Amanda Fox. What I do during these mental indignities is remain myself but become absolutely, rigidly mute. In a winter alone in the wilderness, plainly and simply I would go mad.

Jack balances his antipathy to wolves with a liking for bears. In all his career, his only dangerous experiences with them were walking on several round trips on a path alongside the Finlay River, waist-high in brush and forested with twelve-foot-high cottonwood trees, where two sows and four cubs lived. Another of his Finlay River stories concerns Eric Smallstead, Ben Cork's partner, who was killed on their trapline in a narrow gulch by a snowslide. The grizzlies found him first, after he'd partly melted out of the snow in the spring, and in pulling him out the rest of the way, they tore him in half, because his snowshoes had caught. They didn't eat him, but since the wolverines would have, Jack Lee and Ben Cork put the remains underneath a pile of rocks and got word out to the police on the next month's mail boat about where they could find him. (The Mounties always went up and looked, to prevent homicides.)

A dry snowslide, on an existing crust, is as silent as an owl's whoosh, or like a whisper, and thus more dangerous. At night the first thing you know about it, you feel it trapping you around your legs. A dry slide will divide around the trees, but a heavy, wet, spring avalanche bowls them over with its bulk, and roars like a forest fire, or booms like thunder. Prospecting now is mostly done by helicopters descending into a draw and two vacationing college boys jumping out and taking water and soil samples for an hour or two, for later analysis in a lab. In the old days, it was that a guy would climb into every hole in an entire mountainside he was interested in, shoo out the mountain lions, and crawl back deep into the black and hack off some samples of rock.

There's something so concrete and downright and assertive about a man who's come into his own, is in blooming shape and on his own blessed territory—as Jack is on this trip—that the sight of him has come to irritate me slightly. At home, back on the Kispiox, he's so much less harsh and swaggering, and just *says* less. Unless he's being boyish and musical, his voice here is rather grating, though he talks with considerable effort to find the right words. The difficulties of being partners alone with somebody for the seven least snowy months out in the bush begin to seem plain. We sit by the blowing fire, speckled with ash. Wally Love is cheerful and peaceably amenable, by contrast, while Bill, his brother, is the extrovert—though he was shot through the leg by a hunter they were guiding once, whose bullet continued on through the chest of another client beyond. Then he lost two fingers the next winter, which were caught in a winch, which hurt even more. They'd killed a bear that was scarred end to end with pus pockets and had little chunks or shards of shale embedded everywhere in its skin—must have fallen over a cliff, or been driven off. Bears fight around a tree, the weak one on the far side, using it as a shield.

Billysticks are the sticks you poke on a slant into the ground next to a fire and from the upper end of which you hang your stewpot. Otherwise you cut two posts with crotches in them and put a crosspiece between. Slice shavings with a jackknife and blow the fire up. There is a lot of whisky talk about "niggers" in a hunting camp—greenhorn hunters being that type—and a lot of affectionate "cocksucker" talk, they say. What the guides like Jack or Wally on a hunting trip are really packing into the bush are those guys' braincases, those heads on the *hunters* (not the moose), who pay for the pleasure of charley horses and smoky memories. And Jack is the real thing—a frontiersman, who walked the walk on the vanished trails.

JUNE 28

The exuberant friendship and openness of the last day. My carping mood was gone; I was properly grateful. The plane was due at 6 AM, so we began waiting at 4 AM. The sunrise shone for only a moment. Then Wally stretched out on the grass again to sleep, like a farmer boy. When you're expecting to go, you're ready to go; you're primed for it, but in this country, with its weather combinations, pilots often don't arrive on the day they are scheduled to. Sometimes they don't arrive at all. One of the helicopter pilots I knew in Atlin two years ago was killed last year in a crash; and one of the pilots in Fort St. James was lost for fifty-nine days a few months ago and froze off the fronts of his feet.

As it got towards dusk, Jack cut wood for a long siege—night wood. He hits the log with the blunt end of the blade of the axe first to knock it free of the rest. He's been smoking his chewing tobacco again. You "develop a nerve for smoking" that gets hungry for it, he says; and tells me how to do a moose call—*Goff*—tells me that once, when he'd killed a moose, he was so hungry he drank the blood from its cut throat just in order to collect the strength to skin it and butcher the meat and pack it on home. Frances talks about doctor-hunters who make her cook the brains of their mountain goats, and a customer who drowned in a steelhead stream when his waders filled.

I dreamt of "Negroes" and telephone bells and, while lying awake, repeated my own published words to myself, full of anticipation of leaving the bush. The tent swayed and creaked in the wind like a ship, the rain making a sound like wax paper crinkling. It's been a bleakly high valley to camp in: no pack rats and other jolly animate memorabilia. There aren't even earthworms in the earth, which is a putty-yellow. At 8:30 the next morning, when we were still glumly clinging to our beds with our energy gone, the plane suddenly arrived, circling twice. Then—having waited an extra day—we hurry-hurried, like in the army. The pilot, a saturnine, quiet "half-breed" with a blocky face and a clippered hair cut—a stolid face like a dogsled driver's—gunned it down the lake and swayed away. He had been socked in for two days at the village of Stewart, over by the ocean, en route to Telegraph Creek, and then had flown on from the Stikine to us. No apologies; because this is the way fog works.

It's still the most exciting ride in the world. We look down on kettle-hole ponds and little waterfalls and looping rivers, grey-green, or elephant coloured, and flat-topped mountains smeared with snow, but not high enough to hold glaciers. Crossing Lawyers Pass, we could look straight ahead at Tatlatui Lake through the bee's-wing blur of the propellers. Kitchener Lake and Trygve Lake bracket Kitchener Crag, and Thutade is tucked into a wedge driven into the packed mountains. These three are the headwaters of the Finlay, creamy with rapids where they debouch, though the Firesteel is a big, glassy tributary. Then real snow ranges intervene, with long avalanche-bruised slopes that have been swept stubby or clear by the winter's slides. We do lots of jiggling in the air, the wind's so tough. Though it's a sodden day, fortunately the grey ceiling is high, and every sixty miles comes another vast valley, such as the Sustut's, or the upper Skeena, furred a savage green. Moses Lake is yellow-green, very high and cold, splayed-out so it hardly looks like water. Behind it are tumid, high, jumbly mountains, like Shedin Peak, deep with glaciers or snow.

A jagged brown saw-edge range stands across the way, very massive and too steep to hold much snow. These build higher and higher, thicker too, two peaks deep, until we break through an immense east-west line of meringue-piled cloud shapes to lower country, which is brailed with meadowy creeks, Robin Hood–green—bow and arrow country again. Birches and poplars, but still plenty of arctic black-green. The pilot flies tensely, without sureness or brilliance, wearing an expression of listening. Man is a wolf of the air. Babine Lake appears, but we fly over two more bulky ranges, Cronin and Dome, powdered with snow. "How's that for summer, eh?" he says finally with a laugh.

On the ground they call Lee "Old Trapper," or "Old-Timer," which pleases him, except for the "Old"—he winces at that and turns away.

So we've lived to fly another day! And so ends the centrepiece of this summer. It's fifteen degrees warmer in Smithers. We'd missed two meals at the end, while waiting for the plane, and I'm sick in my tummy and throat.

JUNE 29

Travelled with several country cousins eastward on the train. A grandpa is giving his five grandkids quarters to remember him by. At least, I think they were quarters; maybe they were only nickels—anyhow, they seemed to do the job. There aren't very many young women extant in these parts. All of them of course are married—lean, gopher-shaped, gawky young ladies with sharp eyes and limited spans of attention. There are so few that marriage must seldom be truly a matter of falling for someone, but rather you take what you get and make the best of a necessary partnership in pioneer territory.

I watched the sumptuous June countryside pass—loose horses—and glutted myself with newspapers, the jabber and bicker of journalism, and all of the hectoring sadness of America. If I were more enterprising, I would do a story on some of the Vietnam draft resisters I see in these railroad towns, working in warehouses. They all look shaggily bearded, and like they do have a sense of humour; look *simpatico*. They've gone bushy; they live bunkhouse-style, reading the classics, perhaps.

I've been chasing a priest named Father McCormick across the North. He flies to Fort Ware occasionally, and might have given me a ride. I missed him in Fort St. James on my first day there. Yesterday, just as we landed in Smithers, he, in his Super Cub, took off. Then my train reached Burns Lake, a lovely place, an hour after he'd left *there,* and passed his little red float plane moored at the Lejac Indian School, where we *didn't* stop, and left me at the Vanderhoof station one day ahead of his arrival. So I'm now in Fort St. James once again, a Saturday.

JUNE 30

L.R. Dickinson, General Merchant, and general good guy, wasn't drunk today, so I talked to him. He says it's true he's not drunk, but says he fought in World War I and they didn't drink buttermilk then. And they practically lived on cigarettes. Like so many second visits paid to an informant, this time doesn't work as well. For both of us, the enthusiasm has somewhat wilted and what he tells me is scattered facts. Bob Watson, eighty-four, who was incoherent in the hospital in Vanderhoof, died last week from diabetes and has been taken to Manson Creek for burial. He says the lower Telegraph Trail was called the Black-water Trail, because it ran beside slow, black, fertile rivers, rich in big fish. In the upper part of Stuart Lake, eight hundred to one thousand sturgeon are caught on occasion, but no one has succeeded in finding their spawning grounds. The Indians used to come back with their dugout canoes loaded with them. He says on Dominion Day a tug-of-war was a must: Whites-versus-Indians. The Indians, some of whom earned their living rowing scows up from Quesnel on the Fraser and Nechako rivers, usually won; and several whites would sprain a ligament. The key to it was having an anchor man who could hold fast until the other side played out, and then the rest of you could jerk them over the handkerchief that was laid on the ground for a marker. The Chilcotin Indians, from west of Quesnel, had used to raid way up as far as these Indians' territory and destroy their camps. The Chilcotin Indians and the Nass Tsimshian band were the tough ones. Jimmy Blackwater, a Nass River man, like Thomas Abraham, the Bear Laker, had every seven-year-old that he knew pack 30 pounds on the trail.

He says Irish Sutton was a gentleman with money from the Old Country. Had spent two years at Trinity Medical College, till something changed his life. Wandered across the ocean and hit this country, took to drinking, which he died of—used to drink with John Prince, and traded furs;

Dickinson met him in 1909. And Johnny the Jew "was an old Jew, first a guide in Michigan, worked here in logging camps, had a cabin on the river. He died in a Jewish home in Vancouver." Dickinson says they wanted to send him to Jerusalem, but "old Johnny had been away from it too long; didn't think it was a good idea."

He says in the early days you didn't ask a person his name. Then if he told you, you weren't sure whether that was his name or not. There was a guy who'd shot somebody in the States, and he ran all the way up to the Headless Valley country of the Nahanni River, in the Yukon, where the Mounties turned him back. Came through here, another time, and nearly shot yet another guy. A baker from Scotland was another name-changer; had a bank account in Hazelton, but he couldn't remember in which name he had deposited it. And a lot of men just disappeared. Johnson, a grizzly hunter, and two partners were found dead in their cabin on the Nation River, with signs of vomit on the floor. And Ed Moore's partner, in the Bear Lake country, vanished while on a trip out for supplies. Ed—who'd been in Barkerville and Dawson City for those strikes—waited till he himself was down to skin and bones before coming out. "They hated to leave a claim, you know," he explains, lest somebody jump it, or, hiking through, pick up a nugget.

After a certain number of stories, Dickinson feels he's reached the point of rumour and conjecture, and therefore clams up. Alex Rosen, by contrast, hooted bombastically when he saw me and invited me in to have a beer. He said he'd thought I'd be in California by now. "How's your book going?" he asked. When I stuttered, he laughed. "Not so well, eh?" He says Bob Watson had a workings at Kildare Gulch. A man can't dig after he's eighty, but Bob liked just to sit among his rocks and admire the scenery. He was a middle-class, well-educated fellow, a single-minded prospector, who seldom spoke but always dug up a few bits of gold to live on. A tough one, he could carry one hundred pounds on his back, though he only weighed 165. Rosen says Bob finally drove to Portland, Oregon, saying he'd get the hell out of here, it was too crowded, but came back.

Rosen remembers Irish Sutton as a remittance man, drinking rum and buying furs. And Luke Fowler as "a wise Indian; he knew all the answers." Usually when I ask about an Indian, though, he says, "No savvy him. He was an Indian!" As for Johnny the Jew, "Johnny introduced himself as Johnny the Jew, wasn't backward about it"—Rosen laughs—"Something of a philosopher, fished behind his cabin for hours. Did he come from Chicago?" He tells me again about his own claim, on Pelly Creek. The valley is maybe a couple of miles wide. Limestone sidehills, a few rabbits to snare, a little fishing, for what he calls "mud trout," or char. A little bit of metal there, too, maybe; some mineralizations—though he never had his samples assayed—thought it was lead and maybe zinc. Didn't pay much attention, just kept going. In those days gold was worth only twenty dollars an ounce, and placer gold only sixteen dollars, being mixed with silver or copper. So you had to hustle.

When I asked about the Omineca River, where I'm going, he said, "Oh, just an ordinary stream"—the pokiest river he's ever been on. He rafted down it and had to stick close to the shore to pole himself along, the current was so slow. One time he heard about a new placer find forty miles down from him, and rafted there. It wasn't the deal he'd hoped for, but since he'd built himself a good raft, he decided to keep on floating. So he sat on his pack and rolled smokes, looking at the moon, as he slid along. He'd been told that he'd have to tie up once—when he came to an island that presaged a canyon—but he'd forgotten about that. He even heard rushing water ahead of him, but thought it was sweepers, low-hanging trees, and so steered to the middle of the river to avoid them. The island slipped by before he remembered what it was supposed to represent. He hit the canyon, and a rock in the middle overturned him. He went down, down, and thought that he'd never come up, but at last he did, right next to his raft, by chance, and climbed on again, and paddled safely to shore, and dried out his eiderdown, camping for two days.

JULY 1

The lake is stunning in the perfect sunlight of these exceptionally long days. The sun sets a little before 11 PM and by 4 AM it's what you'd call broad daylight outside. Fort St. James is still easygoing, off-the-beaten-track, and pleasantly relaxed in atmosphere in the morning—all light, all friends.

Albert Alexander tells me he went over to Billy Steele's house for a lesson in reading and writing, as a boy, every couple of weeks—just as his mother and grandfather had done before him. The granddad had moved up from Stuart Lake to Manson Creek when he got rights to a trapline there, though Billy had predated even him. Chief Thomas Abraham, Peter John, and the Alexander family used to take forty to fifty head of horses over west to Takla Landing in the spring, with their furs, after having gone east to the Finlay during the winter with several toboggans and their dogs. In 1928 he listened to his first radio—six feet wide, with earphones—there at Fort Grahame. They'd buy a five-gallon tin of overproof rum for Christmas, and come home. Not in his lifetime, he says, have the Indians been cheated by white men. In 1942, it was sixty-eight below on the Finlay one time. They got home and found Tommy Perkins, who skidded logs with his mother for a living, laid up in bed and fireless. They cut him half a cord of wood, and he gave them some dandelion wine and some resin wine. To make resin wine you put sugar and a yeast cake in a bowl of tree resin and put the stuff in back of the stove for a month or more (eighty or ninety degrees), till it turns liquid. A dentist once came to Manson and did his work out underneath the Jack pines with a foot-pedal drill.

Father McCormick turns out to be thin, thirty-five, grave, and hollowed-out-looking in the face, but healthy, and with a sliding, removable smile, a boy's sort of smile. He's from Prince Edward Island, and likes Indians, is intelligent, adventurous, idealistic, and has a blue, ascetic tint to his face. The bones stand out, but he is inconspicuous in a group, gets along with everyone, wears check shirts. He says generally, in his Oblate Order, they are too occupied to argue much about Pope John XXIII's recent changes in the liturgy, or issues like chastity, etc. Their vows as monks preclude marriage, in any case, and the poverty is assumed, as well. Says perhaps some priests could marry, though. He fidgets a good deal as he talks about it, hides his crotch with his knees; both our eyes are going there.

He says that Fort Grahame had one family, Keom Pierre's, until 1967, but the Ingenika River settlement had been abandoned a couple of years before then. He says at Fort Ware there are perhaps 120 Indians, plus the trader, Art Van Somer, and his wife and kids, and a Mrs. Koul, a sixty-year-old, forceful schoolteacher, and an American Pentecostal missionary and his wife, who've been there three years or so. The Fox Lake, the Paul River, and the

Akie River former village sites each have single Indian families left living in them through the winter. These Finlay River Sikannis are his favourite Indians, the simplest in their customs and the happiest. They speak a different language from this Carrier tribe, on Stuart Lake. The Babine Indians do, too, and they also look different— are squatter, shorter, huskier, and have bigger lips. The word for "moose" on Babine Lake is almost the same as the word for "man" on Stuart Lake. Topley Landing, on Babine, has about fifty Indians living there. Old Fort has only Joe Alex and his family of four. But Fort Babine has about one hundred. Oblate House, his redoubt, is the halfway point on the walk he used to take to Takla Landing from Fort Babine. Takla Lake still has about 150 Indians on it, while Buckley House, another old trading post, has only Johnny French's family of fifteen. And upper Stuart Lake, at the other end from where we are, altogether has maybe three hundred natives, all told. He loves his work; sleeps anywhere; bums meals; adventures abound.

I had a session of banter with Joe Hoffman, trying to get stories out of him, but he wouldn't tell. He has a dark, long, battered, humorous face that you trust. He says that Billy Stack was a short, assertive, humourless, rather unpleasant fellow, a loner, except good to his dogs. Always had a lot of mining pipes around that he'd appropriated from abandoned diggings. He says Bear Lake Charlie shot Hugo Stahlberg through the arm, crippling him—bushwhacked him. And Art Blair was another fellow on the Finlay; went up to the White River in a big punter with a ton of supplies every fall. He'd been a mess sergeant in the US Army, and was said to have absconded with his company's funds.

A girl with Queen of Sheba bangs walks by. Nearly all the men, though, and most of the ladies over thirty have holes in the middle of their faces, where their front teeth have fallen out. In the bar, I hear French and Carrier Indian spoken, not English—Carrier sounds rather like Polish. And there is an old, shiny fellow like Don Quixote with white hair and black eyebrows and a shaking mouth, with an amused expression, and a carved willow walking stick. They taxi in groups about town, like in a communal Turkish taxi, carrying their groceries home, and look quite a bit like Turks.

JULY 2

Gold was discovered by Twelve-Foot Davis on Arctic Creek, off the Omineca River, near Germansen Landing in 1869. Vital Force was also an early bird at Manson Creek nearby, and by 1871 the rush was in full swing. Cataline, the horse-packer, Rufus Sylvester, and Dancing Bill Lapham—proprietor of the "Mad House" honky-tonk there—were other figures.

I alternate, in the same day, periods of intensive, joyful interviewing with lonely, spinning near-despair: this from being so alone. Today I was over at Dickinson's comfortable home, looking at photograph albums. He's got pictures of the hockey and lacrosse teams he played on in the Chilcotins' Cariboo country in 1911, and the diamond drilling he did at Germansen Landing in the 1920s. (The bartender was the goaltender.) And of Peter Himadam himself—an emotive, untidy-looking man, like a Neapolitan organ grinder. And a red-headed commercial traveller, quite an old card, he says, with mutton chop whiskers, who suffered a heart attack beside his long boat. (Dickinson speaks of it as though it were a battle wound.) And there's Cap Hood, the riverman—appearing like a big gross fellow of three hundred pounds, the fat folding around his sarcastic mouth, his belt high up under his chest, and a sagging suitcoat. And little Billy Steele, with a crewcut, a long nose, a malign-looking face, a little moustache. And the stern, dependable, workhorse Indian wife of an early Hudson's Bay trader. And Cataline's famous pack train of fifty-plus horses, the predecessor of George Byrne's on the Telegraph Trail. And Jimmy Alexander, a tall, raffish-looking central figure, with a curved pipe, long arms, a flat-brimmed hat, husky legs; looks rough and ready to go to work in an instant. My friend Frank Swannell, in 1911, has a matinee-idol's moustache, and wears a bandillero of bullets. And his Chinese cook is there, with a little, round, bandit's face, unsteady about the eyes, like an Old South Negro's, subject to slavery. There are pictures of wintering camps, and human pyramids that they used to form on Sundays for fun, after the tug-of-war, and the World War I outfit Dickinson went overseas with. Then there's a late picture of Swannell with some of his shawled lady friends, looking like a plumped-out old roué and showman, a crude P.T. Barnum. And a whole three dozen "clooches" grouped complaisantly about a teamster's trading wagon, dark and giggly in their Hudson's Bay blankets. And an Indian camp—at "John Prince's second trapline layover," on the Nation River—with a white fly and tent, pots, beaver skins stretched on round frames, and beaver meat and trout, out drying on racks.

Sex between races is a universal phenomenon; Romeo was perhaps a "squaw man." And a flock of flying geese sound like a barking, travelling dog team anywhere. I've wanted to relate all this stuff to the great world outside, stewing convulsively in its furies, but it seems too sharp a contrast. Everything is too disparate, with King and the Kennedys newly dead and these historic old-guys from another century alive. Instead I'm taking a respite from the world we all live in and busying myself only with the facts of what is here. I'm not a mixed-media man, either, so although I brought a camera for the first time in my life on any trip, I've never used it till this weekend. Finally I pulled it out and began snapping log cabins, the only subject I've taken so far, lining the boxes up in my sights, after vaguely setting the mechanical dials, and pushing the clicker down. Then when I get home I'll wrestle for words to describe them. Not that one must wrestle; they're simply turtle shells—old, lovely, muddy, stationary brown turtle shells.

JULY 3

Tonight, again, to the house of the combative, retired policeman, Cochran, and heard more of the Indians' evil deeds. He has a rupture which keeps poking out, making him hold his belly with both hands. He's so tough he's likable, with his open blue eyes behind thick glasses, and a lively manner, kicking the floor with his heels for emphasis. He sucks his dental plates almost continually, so that his mouth looks as if what he's saying has put a very bad taste in it, indeed.

He came in just after World War i, he says, to farm. There was lots of good land but no market—you had to eat all the potatoes yourself. There was Hugo Stahlberg bushwhacked. There were two Germans shot on the Finlay—Shorty Webber put through the ice, and Hugo left weeping all night where he lay, until the Sikanni discovered him the next morning. Then there was Frank Johnson, who was a loner, and who especially disliked the Indians. He would shoot at them to scare them, not in order to hit them, but if he did hit one, he said, then he would hang him in a tree as a warning for the rest of them. When Frank disappeared, in 1942, they found his dog nearly starved to death at his cabin, and a pot of beans on his stove that was burned down to nothing. Other people said it was a grizzly, and said that Frank had developed an absolute obsession about bears. But Cochran says Indians. "If our Indians had the get-up-and-go of your niggers in the States, they'd have swept us clean out of the country by now!"

Ed Moore's was another story. He was sick and unfit to travel, so when they'd nearly run out of supplies, his part-ner took the one dog they had left and the sled, but never was seen again—though the dog turned up afterward in the Bear Lakers' Indian band. When Moore was near dead himself, he set out for Takla Landing. He'd snared two or three rabbits near the cabin that saved his life for a while, and finally was found by the Thomas Abraham bunch of Bear Lakers, crawling on all fours in the snow. They were amused and they stripped him of his gear and what money he had. He kept promising them that he would pay them five hundred dollars if they carried him at least to Takla Landing, where whites could help him—while they par-leyed and parleyed about it in their own tongue. They had their own pidgin lingo, made up of the languages of the several tribes that they were remnants of, and although they were on their way somewhere else, they did turn around and save him. He never paid them, however, because he believed that they had killed his partner.

I went to talk to Olaf Hogberg, who summers in Joe Hoffman's row of apartments. After forty years here, he still has a strong Swedish accent. He's a teetotaller because he saw a family ruined by drinking as a child, which keeps him away from other Swedes, he says. He has a staunch, light-filled face, an intelligent, sunburned forehead, handsome in the way of a handsome professor's, somehow. He made a hairy sleigh trip from Finlay Forks to Germansen Landing, and back, on the river ice for grub during the winter of 1932, and when he wintered in Fort St. James, he and his brother used to each pull in four hundred pounds of stuff in the fall on little sleighs, on snowshoes. Then they'd "turn on the water," in the sluice boxes, at their claim at Finlay Forks about May 1st. He's a very outspoken guy, so for the first time I'm hearing some unattractive stories of Billy Steele that other people just hinted at. Steele was friendly to the Indians of the particular band his girlfriends came from, and he would buy gold nuggets from them, as well as their furs. He seemed also particularly friendly to greenhorns. When Olaf first arrived, he told Olaf that if he cut wood for him for six days Billy would take him out and show him a fine prospect where he could stake a claim. But then at the end of those days, when Olaf brought up the subject, he said he was busy—"you work for another six days for me." And yet he was good to his dogs, pointing out that they're much warmer than a sleeping bag—he'd have seven or eight on the bed with him, if he hadn't a squaw. Often he promised Olaf a nugget about the size of a brown bean—"when you leave"—in return for various favours he asked of him. He'd showed it to him many times, but of course never did come through with it in the end. And once, when he'd injured his hip, six of them took turns packing him something like forty miles to Germansen Lake, where a plane could land. However, when they got there, as if to deliberately aggravate them, Billy Steele said he had some traps placed round about that he wanted to see to while he was able, before the plane came, and he limped off and took care of all that. Another time—when he was drunk, at the twenty-first birthday party of a girl who was visiting her mother—he got jealous with regard to the mother's attentions and began shooting his .45. They tricked him and grabbed him away for the night, tied him up, threw water on him, and so on. His revenge was to take ten dollars from them, for registering a claim the next year, but kept the ten dollars and didn't register it—instead registered it for friends of his—telling them, when they came back, that they were only imagining they'd asked the errand of him.

Bob Watson, who just died, was a former RCMP in the Peace River country, but quit after some kind of misunderstanding and walked in all the way from there. He was a "sniper," a guy who was a great walker but never actually had any claims of his own, just snatched nuggets from other people's creeks as he trekked through. You never knew quite where his gold bits originated from. He'd sell them at the bank real quick and hike out again. He had been in the Queen's Own Rifles from 1915 to 1918.

John Smith was the "town waterworks" in Fort St. James, delivering water to the houses from a barrel on a truck drawn by an old nag. And Olaf's former prospecting partner, named Erickson, was "a shipwrecked Swede who married a native princess." But, "Steer clear of the Indians unless you want to join the tribe," says Olaf. "If you want to sleep at night you steer clear. Otherwise a knock comes on the door around two, and you gotta get up and give them all a drink!"

A little man named Ogilvie walked like a rabbit—walked forty miles in a day without a pack, although with a pack he could hardly go ten. He was an engineer, and a lover-boy with other people's wives in town, and had been mixed up with a scandal involving salting gold prospects in the Barkerville region before selling them to greenhorns. He was on Slate Creek, working for the Consolidated Mining Company, and was a bullheaded old bugger. He once corduroyed a road for many miles straight through a swamp that he ought instead to have gone around. Some places it was built up four feet off the muskeg, so that very shortly it collapsed.

Douglas Lay was the chief government engineer, and Olaf spent two months, and Cochan four months, in packing him throughout the country and being cook-and-bottle-washer for him. They had only a handful of horses, so there was usually nothing to do but pan a little gold, if you felt like it, while Lay conscientiously visited every claim in the country, sketching the strata. He was a scrawny little fellow, a brilliant geologist, ungrumbling, but one-fourth of a pound of tea was enough for only about three cups for him, he liked it so strong.

Billy Martin, a friend of Art Hyndman's, was packed out with rheumatic fever, but Billy conned his sister, a Mrs. Tait, for money by leaving his diaries behind, then "selling" them to her. A former policeman from California named Harding was a crack pistol shot. Ralph Meissener, also a crack shot, had had an unlucky love affair and fled to the bush for seven years. He never said a thing unless he absolutely had to. He was Olaf's partner part of the time, and an easygoing troubleshooter in emergencies, but a silent partner, never a word if he didn't have to. Dick Corliss, a freighter on the Crooked River at first, became a bush pilot when the planes came in. Archie King stuttered, and was a bootlegger. Ed Moore would hold a grudge for fifteen years, but otherwise always was good for a laugh at suppertime. A teamster named Skinner took dynamite as well as oats and hay on his regular loads for the mines, but shat his pants once, when he lost control with a half ton of dynamite in the wagon while going downhill. Shot two of his horses to stop the skid—since the wagon couldn't run over them—but never lived down having to change his pants. He carried a fiddle.

Agate Alexander had begun to take on a squaw's squat shape by the time Olaf knew her. He used to feed her sometimes, when he cooked at a little mining camp as a greenhorn and she stopped in. She supplied moose and caribou meat to them all at ten cents a pound, and the boss bet Agate fifteen dollars once that she couldn't get him a caribou's hindquarters by tomorrow, because she would have had to walk so far to the hunting grounds he knew she would never be able to do it. But she brought sixty-seven pounds' worth in in good time, having killed that particular caribou previously, with foresight. Olaf once shot a grizzly bear which had kept Agate up in a tree all night, walking circles around it. Then he gave her the hide, because it weighed ninety-two pounds and the freighter charged ten cents a pound to take things out. Olaf had a .321 Browning automatic and a .300 Savage rifle, "like firing through Billy Steele's stovepipe." And Olaf walked sixty-seven miles in two days from the Nation River, after a man was hurt in a sawmill accident—including sixteen hours non-stop. He just grabbed all the lunches that the men had there and headed out to get help; took no blankets. Frank Johnson—another great walker—went sixty-two miles in a single day. He had a bottle of gold nuggets and dust cached behind a stump, which he showed Olaf in case he disappeared. Eventually he *did* disappear, but Olaf hasn't been back into that country since to collect the bottle. Frank hated the Indians for reasons in his own character, and because he'd caught them stealing his beaver. He was six foot two, hunted and hated the wolverines and wolves, but named all the grizzlies who were around, and would shoot only the old white-faces. He was an educated man, with some secret or other in his background, and one time he caught pneumonia in his cabin, fourteen miles from the sawmill camp, and, harnessing his three dogs to the sleigh, and drinking coal oil to keep his circulation up (it acts like alcohol), simply allowed them to carry him there. He stayed eight or nine days, getting well, before rushing home to his claim before some "sniper" like Bob Watson robbed him blind.

Peter Jenson was the fellow at McConnell Creek, on the cutoff, who sheltered the Gitksan outlaw, Gunanoot. He got along well with the Indians, and kept a little store, as every prospector with an outgoing personality did, like Ben Cork also. But he'd bury his valuables in a tin box under the woodpile when he went away for a while, and leave his door unlocked so that they wouldn't break it down. Luke Fowler was another aging old-timer with a reputation in the early thirties. He had become a scrounger by then. He'd roamed so far out from Hazelton that he never had a chance to pack in much grub, and Olaf, at the cook shack, would save all of the uneaten breakfast hotcakes, and Luke would come once a week and collect them and go off a couple of hundred yards, across the field, and eat them quietly, or as many of them as he could eat. He also was "long-fingered" in regard to bacon or liquor.

Ah Luck, the Chinaman, arrived in 1886 and left in 1934. He made over three thousand dollars every year, but when he accumulated that much he would leave for Vancouver. He had a squaw, who left sometimes to return to her people, but otherwise packed supplies eighty miles from Takla Landing on her back for him, even àt sixty-eight, and with a papoose on top, when she'd had a papoose. Ah Luck sold turnips and rutabagas and carrots at ten cents a pound in the ground—you dug them out—also early rhubarb at fifteen cents a pound, which he forced in the spring by heating rocks and setting them in a circle in the snow around his patch.

Cataline, who was a Spaniard, had two hundred horses in his train at one time, and campsites every fifteen miles on the Telegraph Trail. By 1892 there were a thousand Chinese working these mines—which predated the Klondike strike—and an upright piano was freighted from Hazelton by dog team.... As for Skook Davidson, he left town in 1941 for the Kechika River, with Craig Forlar and Frankie Cook, two teenage boys, and a grey horse from Vanderhoof in his string which he'd stolen and painted black. But, on the other hand, he repaid a five-hundred-dollar loan from Olaf's brother on the brother's deathbed. These fatherly, kidding old bachelors, Olaf and Rosen, really open up as their logjam of prudent silence breaks.

But the happiest days in Olaf's life, he tells me, were when he was travelling in northern Italy after the war with two Americans who'd left their tour and three girls they'd picked up. ("No orangutan about them at all.")

JULY 5

As Bruce Russell says, the Americans have taken over the North without firing a shot. The choicest property is being bought up, and now here I am, after even the myths. These people do want their history recorded, however, so they must take the historian that's offered, New Yorker and stutterer though he is. As I did back on June 16, six times I've walked to Jack Thompson's house, because of the wash hung out on the lines, but apparently that was only a trick so people would think he was in town—that and the unmade bed. He's been in Manson Creek all the time. Bruce Russell is the trucker who goes clear to Uslika Lake (these names are a cross between real Indian names, and surveyors' joke-names), which is 190 miles north of Fort St. James, about a fifteen-hour, one-way trip, if all goes well, and he is Thompson's competitor. Last weekend he trucked Bob Watson's body up for burial, performing the service there himself. About thirty people showed up, he says, which is most of the residents of the Manson Creek area. The only ones who didn't show were Watson's immediate neighbors, from across the creek, who of course had feuded with him, as bachelor neighbors will.

They did get as far as the store, but couldn't bring themselves into the graveyard.

Russell is a sweet-natured, tenor-voiced man, who reminds me very much of my college roommate. He's dogged and dusty, humble, appealing, a forgetter, and a bit of a battler. He has a trucker son and a schoolteacher son and is a grandfather, although he looks forty. He licks his lips a lot; doesn't charge anyone for their freight if they are poor. A big Canadian Freightways trailer-truck rig comes in regularly, leaving the full trailer in his lot and pulling away an empty one. He speaks of that delivery as "the dog team." He has a picture in his living room of Cataline, his great Spanish predecessor on the mining route. As a matter of fact, Skook first worked for Cataline, packing on the Telegraph Trail, and got his nickname, "Tough," from the Hazelton Indians after a barroom brawl. Cataline sits looking at the camera in front of a brick wall. He has a shapeless body, a very large head, a thick downward-U moustache, big, ugly hands, and long, black, balding hair. He's wearing a rumpled, dirty, silk neckerchief, and a black, shiny, costume-like jacket, with a few metal buttons showing. He's got an oath-shouting face, a villainous brute of a face with depressions under the cheeks and sagging eyes, a big forehead, and a huge area underneath that, deep lines from his nose paralleling his moustache. It's a water buffalo's face. He never wore socks, only leather boots, and never used more than one blanket in the winter, Russell says.

Russell's wife is a "cultured" woman, and therefore feels married to something of a brute. She flirts with me, as we sit together on a chunk of cool agate, and affects Scandinavian dress. She wears pigtails, a little red necktie, cut-off blue jeans, and her dog seems trained to viciousness. She speaks of London's Bow bells, and finds artifacts in her backyard, such as spearheads, tinderboxes, axe heads, a moose-scrotum container for gun powder. A Hudson's Bay post was run like a ship, with an official Carpenter and Blacksmith, who cut their initials on what they made, so we take note of those. She is said to sleep around during her husband's gruelling drives north, and he supposedly has been known to shack up with an Indian maiden up Manson way, but their marriage isn't lacking in joking affection, either. His father was a harness-maker, which was a dying trade. The poor fellow had to move west by stages in order to keep up with the last embers of it, he says.

With some bitter-sounding ironies from Russell to his wife about phoning in the middle of the night to see if she's at home, we set off. Immediately, as we leave and get out on the road, he becomes cheerier. It's nice he's so happy in his work, but too bad he has to work so hard in order to be happy. He's put a hand-lettered sign saying Royal Mail on the front of his truck to keep the tourists out of his way. It's a three-ton truck, new this year but already old, and carries forty-five gallons in its two gas tanks. In the winter he drives a Sno-Cart up every couple of weeks with the mail—a twenty-hour trip, then, to Manson Creek, which is 120 miles. He shovels and clankety-clanks his way along, hauling a sleighload or two of freight behind. *Those* trips are really his pride. On the way up you'll see a moose in a moose yard, and on the way down just his scattered bones. Sometimes he has to unhook the sleigh and break trail ahead with the Sno-Cart alone. The Ed Cosic family wintered twenty-one miles off the road, on the Old Baltic Trail, and they'd hike out once in a while to meet him for their mail, even the seven-year-old girl—going on bear-paw snowshoes the size of his steering wheel. Of course, trapping is rather a put-on now. The trapper is told in the fall he's going to get thirty-five dollars for beaver, and then by the time he comes in in the spring with his pelts the price has "fallen" to twenty-five dollars.

Russell is both pro-Indian and pro-animal. He carries a Polaroid, not a rifle, and he remembers during the Hungry Thirties how many white men the Indians helped. The Indians did pretty well without money because they had gardens and wild meat, and with their lack of money-consciousness, they'd give stuff away. Russell and a friend were playing their accordions at an Indian wedding for a dollar apiece, when things were awfully scraggly and thin, and old Grandfather Alexander just walked over in the middle of it and handed them each a five-dollar tip: which kept them in beans for quite a while. Some Indians are as "honest as the day is long," he says, and some "can't be trusted with a counterfeit dime."

The first mail stop we make is sixty-four miles out, where the Nation River comes purling around a couple of cliffs, neither fast nor slow, from Tchentlo Lake. In 1936, with a truck, he says, this same round trip took five days to make; or if he used horses they got larkspur poisoning, during the summer, and in snowtime got their legs so badly cut up on the crust that the trail turned all blood, and some guy might bring them home later on the sled. We saw a moose calf legging it away, and various spruce grouse, and a snowy owl, mottled in its summer plumage, which looked immense and flapped off from us like a giant moth. Also a little three-year-old grizzly flopping down the road, like a rag on a line in a good wind—his ass high, as a cinnamon bear's wouldn't have been. Russell talks about the earlier days, when they built the road, using two old cars for transport and a wood-burning steam shovel. There was a hairy situation in one place, where the bed of a creek they were trying to cross dropped suddenly into a hole, and the firebox of the steam shovel went under the water. A guy was mauled by a bear, also, but managed to save himself because he had got off one shot first, which had broken the bear's lower jaw—a sow with three cream-coloured cubs. He grew a rabbinical beard after that to cover his facial scars. To protect your cabin from bears nowadays, Russell says, you take

an aerosol bomb and coat it with pork fat and hang it outside. No other animal can get hurt by it, but the local bear
will come along and bite.

I spent two complete days in that truck, though Russell carries only a huge thermos of coffee, which gets older
and older, and colder and colder. The top of the cab is
stuffed with plastic for insulation. It was like the trip up
the Yellowhead route, in central B.C., in 1960, when Amy
and I spent three ten-hour days in second gear, in order
to go about three hundred miles; or the road in to Telegraph Creek from the Alcan Highway. We stopped to chat
with every car (meaning two or three), although Russell
drives without stopping to eat—he lives on cigarettes,
peppermints, and coffee. The robins are singing a Rain
Song, he says. And I'm the gun-bearer; I sit holding two
rifles between my knees which he's packing in for individual miners. He tells me about people's fixations—certain
prospectors for certain sinkholes, and Frank Johnson's
for grizzlies. The people at Germansen Landing recently
lost a horse off the bridge when it was being led behind
a jeep and bolted and hung itself. It fell into the Omineca
among some logs and drowned, though they did cut the
rope. An Indian set a set-gun for a bear at a moose carcass
he hung in a tree, but forgot the next time he walked by.
"But he miss himself." And a white man and woman, who
hadn't their gun with them, drove a bear into a tree, outside Vanderhoof, and the man sharpened a stick, so that

his wife could keep it there while he went home for the gun. For three hours she did this successfully, and he shot it and they filled all their containers with bear lard and oil...Then the stories of "Chinamen," who shipped in real Chinese rice in bamboo baskets to live on, and scowed in one-hundred-pound sacks of fish-meal fertilizer for their vegetable gardens, and packed water way the hell uphill for their sluice boxes, in dry territory, putting the sluice boxes on stilts to give them an extra tilt. They'd tunnelled deep enough into the mountain so industriously they were able to keep working all through the winter.

The shelving and contours on the mountain above Manson Creek show where a river once ran. At a shack on Wolverine Lake lives Louie Alexander, Agate's putative husband, who looks like an "Uncle Tom Chinaman." He was the one who found Luke Fowler dead. We leave off a couple of boxes of goods for him, free of charge, and Russell begins talking pidgin Sikanni to a just-nubile granddaughter, who is there taking care of him, with the insinuating air of a white who has initiated many a girl-of-the-bush before. Louie was a cuckold, etc., but his father was one of the tall, straight, intelligent, old-style Indians of the country, expert trappers and dog men, who could speak French and Cree, having learned from the nineteenth-century wave of fur-chasers.

Manson Creek General Store is now in the possession of a winky, hefty Californian and his wife, who has recessed, shadowy, blind-looking eyes. They're school teachers escaping the rat race of L.A. and are very kind. Like Russell, they don't charge me anything because of the mission I'm on. But I've never seen such a bitey dog as this one. As experienced as I am with dogs, I have trouble with this German shepherd, and even dream about him. "King" has bitten three people so far this summer, they say.

Lots of butterflies. It was tough mining here, says Russell. The overall boss, Dagenau, was a millionaire who had made his money in South Africa, so he worked his employees like African natives. If someone was fired, white or Chinese, he was just given a lunch and made to walk the 120 miles back to Fort St. James. The trucks were forbidden to pick him up. The guy had a bubble-nosed, bass-voiced foreman, who lisped: dark complexion, pocked face. There was no air in the tunnel, and water dripped steadily down. They used carbide lamps, and one time a roof caved in—came in on them—and they lost two men. Placer mining—shaking a gold pan in a creek bed—was infinitely better.

There will be strawberries soon, and, most of all, best of all, black currants, which go into breakfast pancakes and have the most vitamins, Russell says. The first thing he does in the winter, if there's an emergency, is get out of the truck and build up a fire, before he does anything else. Then he digs out, or changes the tire, or sees what he can do about the vapour lock in the heater that has seized up.

We drove and drove, folded into the wilderness like a bug in a rug—past cottonwoods, poplar, spruce, and lodgepole pine. The road was greasy where it was wet, and as dry as rust where it was not. Blocky blue mountains rose to one side, the Wolverines, with snow on the north slopes.

The Omineca, a substantial river famous for gold, is brown and grey-green, and it flows past Germansen Landing so slowly as almost to seem like a stillwater. Besides Dominick Abraham, a benighted son of the Bear Laker chief, Thomas Abraham, only two families live at Germansen. Don Gilliland, a retired game guide, is a lean, ageless fellow with a Scotsman's big nose on his small head. He has a taut, stooped, fast-moving wife, frontier-tough, who runs a café with moosehide on the seats. The walls are covered with cardboard-ink signs specifying how much each type of accommodation costs, what a bath costs, when the generator and thus the light bulbs are on. They're childless and she is his first wife, but she had children before. He's a nice fellow, though he'll say very little to me because he wants to write his own book. His problem with it is that it takes him more days to write down the story of his trail trips than it did to make the trail trips themselves, he says. I agree. He was a house painter, but quit because the fumes affected him; he was allergic to them. He tells me Ben Cork, Jack Lee's friend on the Toodoggone, was the former storekeeper at Fort Ware, and that Shorty Webber became partners with

Hamburger Joe in the late thirties, and both of them were sent to prison for two years for stealing gas for their outboard motors from the airplane-fuel barrels at the mouth of the Ingenika and filling the barrels with water instead (a matter of life or death, perhaps, to the next bush pilot). Shorty learned the trade of a tailor in prison and came back a chastened, reformed, respectable man. Shorty, Hamburger Joe, and Buck Buchanan all worked gold claims on the Ingenika, and all lived with Indian girlfriends, and all rather pulled for the Indians.

The other citizens of Germansen Landing are "The Wilderness Westfalls." Wes Westfall, a transplanted Idahoan, has the face of an oaf grown up, a grown-up Jughead. They give weather reports every three hours, being the only station between Prince George and Dease Lake (an enormous, dizzying stretch of wild land), and relay messages, and refuel planes. Since both the Gillilands and Westfalls rent cabins, I had the choice of staying on the old-timers' side of the river, or staying with mere six-year Canadians, where the action of radio-chat, and pilots landing, and all that is. I stayed with the Westfalls, therefore, in order to try to pick up an airplane ride to Fort Ware, and to give my messages to Steele Hyland, Jack Lee, and so on, all of whom talk on the radio. I have scary, tension dreams, however, as well as girl dreams (though coitus is always prevented), and lack some of the ebullience of the summer of 1966, though my body has proven itself to be as young as ever at walking, or working on the truck, and so forth. In New York, I had become convinced that I'd aged irreversibly, physically; but here I find that that's not the case. Young in body, but aging in mind. It's a painful deprivation to go without hugging a woman for so long. (I laugh to compare this summer with last year, in Aspen, when I had the mountains and those pretty students, besides.) And I want to get on with the business of being a married man, too, of having a child and making a life. And one of the emptinesses in this wild-woods corner of the world is the look of the women. These men, these husbands, go through all of life and never once see a really beautiful woman. Not only have they plain Janes for wives, but they don't see even once a woman as pretty as Marion, and some of the other ladies I've known and loved. Amy, Brigit, Leonore.

Talked to Dominick and Esther Abraham. He says he's Alec Jack's nephew and that he's been to Caribou Hide, Alec Jack's ancestral home, twice, and to Fort Ware: all this twenty to thirty years ago. His looping trapline lies from the Uslika and Aiken lakes to Johanson, one hundred miles square, including the headwaters of the Omineca and the Sustut Rivers. He left Bear Lake, his birthplace, thirty years ago, lived at Takla Landing, and now here, a three-days walk away from Takla and six days from Bear Lake. He has seven grown kids, but they don't come out now from Fort St. James to help him on that arduous trapline. Of his distinguished father, he says, "He's dead." That's what he tells me by way of describing almost anybody. He has eight dogs, and he is going out soon to net whitefish for them, as well as for the Westfalls. There was another Indian woman stopping here with a white husband, who joked about his own "black feet—must be part Siwash." He was a large, unshaven, earthy guy, and she had a heavy laugh, lots of flesh, a big lap, big breasts, shoulders, and stomach, big arms to hug with, and a constant sensuous shifting—altogether a woman well worth living with. The whites were talking about eating snowbirds, owls, and woodpeckers—the first two a delicacy. The Indians don't *like* to crack their cars up, but if they do, they at least get a laugh out of it, and similarly they didn't *want* the Mounties tipping over their barrels of homebrew in the old days, but if it happened, they at least enjoyed the drama of it.

Bruce Russell and I drove all the way through to the end of the road at Uslika Lake, fifty miles farther than Germansen Landing, where there's a lot going on. A dude hunting camp is being built, and a helicopter mining camp. As always, the mining camp is womanless, but the guides' camp has Indian women at it, cooking. There is something bleak and emotionally starved about all of these technological mining camps. Fly-in; fly-out. We had crossed the Osilinka, a raven-black river about seventy feet wide, and nearly reached the Mesilinka, and then met the best people that I've met this summer, at Uslika. They were two "boys" thirty-two and thirty-four, Sam Keene and George Schellenberg, from the Chilcotin country, well south of Vanderhoof. The thirties are the ideal age for doing things, and these are the only guys of about that age who are out doing the doing. Otherwise it's only been old-timers talking of the past.

Sam is a homey, twitchy, thin-faced, rod-thin, active fellow, originally from Wyoming, as skinny as Oliver Twist. Coming up from Wyoming to the Chilcotin stimulated his imagination, and eventually he went on north to Finlay Forks (where these rivers flow in) and worked there for a year—worked also in Fort St. James, and prospected all over the Manson–Germansen Landing area, two summers ago. Last summer, he came back, put on a 135-pound pack and carried it straight through to Fort Ware, past the Ingenika, and the hook of the Finlay, and went on to Fox Lake, and Spinel Lake, and the valley of the sizable Obo River, and then way over to the Chukachida, and back south clear to Kitchener Lake and McConnell Creek. He says that northern country around the hook of the Finlay is very barren of minerals. Finally, he did find a river bar he liked near the head of the Ingenika, a six day walk from here at Uslika Lake. So, he has supplied the claim they are going to be working and the prospecting savvy, and his partner, George, who is a cowboy from the Chilcotin region and is more extraordinary-looking, supplied seven horses—which they've ridden north for five hundred miles already, with their dog Duke running alongside. Dogs here are either called Duke or King, but they earn the titles by the feats they do.

This partner of Sam's, named George, has very large, piercing eyes, very clear, but slightly adrift and crazy-looking. He's all bones; his bulky clothes hang off him—an extreme, alarming boniness—just enough bones to walk with—and evinces extreme deliberation. He talks extremely slowly, in a small, wheezy, reedy voice, though pleasant to the ear—a tiny, tardy voice, which sounds much more "resigned" to life than he really is. He's out here for the experience, the adventure, to "learn something," not especially to strike it rich. He has a pointy little chin, split, scabbed lips, a grey beard, *huge,* grey, aged hands, and an old face—twenty years older than his numerical years, and is marked and wrinkled around the eyes, as if with suffering. Here and there—the forehead, the mouth, and in that extreme boniness, perhaps—he looks his age. But otherwise he looks already seasoned and hardened like a man of fifty. Both are dressed in green shirts, white hats, with strips of caribou skin for a hatband, long, weathered riding boots, and jeans that are grey with rubbed-in dust and wear. They've gone five hundred miles in a month of riding, and have only two months of summer ahead of them, when they can placer-mine. They've got a little Homelite chainsaw, two sluice boxes, some pack boxes, and leather for making pack saddles, a pathetic, inadequate pile of food, a tiny gas pump for lifting a small volume of water out of the river to the tilted sluice boxes (tilted to a sixteen-inch drop), fifty gallons of fuel, and the mining licence, which will permit them to hunt and fish for their living, as well. They also have their coughs: as do I have a morning cough, incidentally, and what a cough! It comes not from germs but from the abrasions of the wilderness, I think. Even two-year-old Duke looks six, at least. He's a slinky fighting dog, golden, except streaked with black, and his ears lie close to his head.

Among their seven horses, they have two "wanderers" that they say they "picked up," and Duke drives in the laggards every morning. The Mesilinka River will be their only formidable swim, and a cable crossing there lifts "the freight" over (a "trolley car," Sam calls it). He's the explorer, but he seems the follower, next to George, who is a real one-in-a-thousand. He's a caterpillar mechanic, when he can get along with other people, he tells me, his walleye drifting, and was born northeast of Swift Current, Saskatchewan—but hasn't seen a good lightning storm since he left the prairies, so he's looking forward to one of those in the mountains, he says. At their present camp they've got a killdeer nest they're watching, as they rest, and some wild peas to eat; also a bridge across the creek to help them track the horses in the morning, and beavers in the cottonwoods, and the clouds in lumps overhead.

Like the grizzlies, these few undiscouragable men of the bush have withdrawn here.

JULY 6

I went next door to Dominick Abraham's again and took some pictures of his old cabin with holes in the roof, that he says belongs to Mr. Westfall. "Grizzly den" has been scrawled contemptuously on the door by whites, who treat it as a sort of sharecropper shack. He has little grand-kids, and his eldest daughter with him now, a girl of an appropriate age and not unattractive, but who wears very baggy chino trousers and has plastered Band-Aids across her forehead, as if to escape attention. They cook on a loaf-shaped stove set outdoors, with a few iron pots. He's put up a tent for the kids, but he says they're too scared to sleep in it. The dogs seem to be in fair shape—six chained sled dogs, and a single yapping bear dog that's loose. The mother sled dog dug a bear-like hole in the bank of the hill overhead for the winter. Dominick keeps a cardboard box full of waste scraps and dried moose tendons for them. Also dry tallow and some jars of moister, moose-oil butter, for his family, and some dried moose noses to cut strips off of, like bacon, and some beaver tails for the same purpose; also intestines for making soup. There are metal hide-scrapers around, and tanning-sticks, a skin stretcher, two beaver traps, a wire marten trap, some wire for making beaver snares, a meat-drying rack over a firepit, and a tanning rack. He showed me a glass jar full of beaver castor, for trapping, flavoured and scented additionally with rum, and a large, clean, white moosehide, too, which would turn yellow when smoked, he said, plus some buckskins; also some Indian withe rope, and coiled white-man's rope.

Two tourist white boys were throwing stones down the hill that hit his roof, and shouting racist insults, and snickering, then hiding, while the Indian family looked up at them anxiously. That was why his grandchildren were scared, Dominick said. "White man do that," he said. But Dominick still busied himself to show me the curiosities he had. All North American Indians, eastern or western, have much the same musical accent to my ear, more like a Mexican's than a Negro's, but of course distinct, and cornered, reviled and impoverished as the Abrahams were, I felt sorry for them.

The remarkable thing about Telegraph Creek, in 1966, was the good humour there, the good relations everybody seemed to have. Here, "The Wilderness Westfalls" push, push for money and business, and the Gillilands, across the river, like an amiable gamekeeper and a crusty housemaid, just keep their head above water and look on, amused. There's no contact. I walk across the bridge for most of my meals, however, for the soft-key Canadian tone of life, though I'm getting no stories from Gilliland. He's intent on saving them for his own book. So I eat radishes, lovely new lettuce leaves, and oven-fried steak in a most valuable silence. I'm reading Bertrand Russell's *Autobiography* and sit by the wild Omineca, which in all its 150 miles (it flows from almost Bear Lake to Finlay Forks) has only this single primitive bridge, and three disparate families living alongside. Once a day or so, a plane comes purring out of the sky with a confident, low-pitched, low-key roar, and refuels by the gravel bar, while Dominick Abraham's chorus of sled dogs bark. The forest is two-thirds white spruce and one-third lodgepole pine and balsam fur. Northward are the black spruce and Jack pine.

Gilliland's new bear hide looks like an alligator, from the flesh side, with its eye holes, sprawled limbs, rutted brown inside-out skin, and haggard eloquence. The Westfalls flew today to the new, instant town of Mackenzie for various ribbon-cutting ceremonies, to get to know people, and I shot a basketball through a bicycle tire at their place.

THE STORY of Fort Ware: Ware, Sr., died, and Ware, Jr., took over, but was eventually fired by Hudson's Bay for being too easygoing with his credit to the Indians (he had naturally married one of them). He stayed around for a while, trapping, and then went south and fell into the saw of a sawmill and died. A Mrs. Copeland became the Hudson's Bay Post manager. Then they closed down the post, and Ben Cork started his own independent store there. The Upriver Boys (north of the Ospika tributary) liked and

married the Indians. The packers passing through, back
and forth, it's said, tolerated them. And the Finlay Forks
group of whites was contemptuous of them and treated
them as though they were blacks.

Baths cost the same as haircuts (a dollar fifty), and it
isn't really kosher to want one too often. I think there's
more of a sneering tone towards the Indians to be heard
from these new Americans than from the old-timers,
who've seen them for so many years and watched their
gradual decline and fall. I notice it when I watch Indians
visit the Gillilands and then go over to the "Wilderness
Westfalls"—how much more relaxed they are at the Gillilands'. The Westfalls treat them with all the jocular cru-
elty they would show to Harlem Negroes.

Ben Ginter, for no known reason, had a car push a mud
track the width of its snowplow blade nearly all the way
to McConnell Creek, so the summer trail there is "open."
Then the car broke down and was abandoned. One of the
pilots yesterday, flying over the Omineca, thought he was
lost because it looked like a big green river from the air
instead of the big brown river he was expecting.

I've found out the basis for the quarrelling relations
between Bob Watson and his neighbor, Johnny Neilson,
of Manson Creek. It was after the death of a man named
Erickson. He had died alone, had grown stiff with rigor
mortis in his cabin, and, without taking measurements,
Johnny Neilson built him a nice coffin, lining it carefully

with a new blanket, and doing good workmanship with the wood for his friend. But it didn't fit, so Bob Watson and Wes Westfall ripped the end out and, in effect, built a new coffin that he could go into, without telling old Neilson they had done this. Then the last straw was when things were being readied for the graveside ceremony, and old Erickson's dog jumped up on the coffin, leaving footprints on the new wood. Johnny Neilson got angry, it being his handiwork, but tough Watson hollered out that that's the last chance the poor dog was ever going to have any contact with his master, and to leave him alone.

Data: To register a placer lease is thirty dollars; a hardrock lease is five dollars; and in either case, you pay a five-dollars-a-year filing fee thereafter for registering your work assessment, and another five dollars for your miner's licence.

JULY 7

The pitch of loneliness, when it comes on, usually in the daytime, is so extraordinarily steep and severe, it takes real control for me to resist—in other words, not to catch an available ride south to Fort St. James and out. Oh, it's a dizzying loneliness; and then a moment's kindness, a kindly chat with somebody, and it's okay for a while again, though every day I'm missing Marion's pregnancy.

Manson Creek, where I am now, is a wide spot in the road without any particular view but very homelike nevertheless, with its several surviving old-timers, and the Los Angeles expatriates, and a couple of other wanderers or lost souls. Big Massey Ferguson mining equipment looms about; gas is seventy cents a gallon. It's a definitely friendly, genial place, however, and the Owens, the Californians, are chiefly responsible for that. They have put up a couple of dozen birdhouses, and don't fuss about money, and provide lots of coffee and what not. They have pretty daughters, named Leslee and Lynnlee, a boy, Evy; the wife is Maggie; his name is Larry. All the creeks around have been worked for perhaps a whole century, but a young Dutchman brought in a specimen bottle today with an inch of gold grains on the bottom which looked like grains of tobacco. He had got them by simply shaking out the mats of old sluice boxes. Larry Owen is something of a father figure round about—a former high school teacher—and Maggie wants some day to write about family life in the wilderness, as Theodora Stanwell-Fletcher did in *Driftwood Valley*, which lies at the head of Takla Lake. She keeps a spiral-ring notebook listing the books she's read in their six winters here. They're the other type of American, compared to the Westfalls—the American who wants a refuge of peace in the wilds, though Larry has one of those large fleshy faces with a lot of lines in it which, when you study it, seem to add up to less.

Johnny Nielsen still has his Swedish accent, although he came into this country thirty years ago, in the spring of 1938, and before that had worked on the timber boats between Florida and New York. Says "you see" at the end of each sentence, and speaks in a rush like a high-pressure faucet, then turns it off. He worked on Twenty Mile Creek and six other claims. He lives here in Skook Davidson's old cabin, which was later Fred Aslin's store. The flooring is composed of boards that were originally used for the shelving. He wears a mechanic's brown pants and shirt, and likes to scandalize you—say that people were "cocksuckers," but then seems to cut himself off. He says that Ed Moore was on Germansen Lake; they called him Horseface Moore, and he always carried a crooked pipe. Billy Steele, 1870–1953, the sub-mining recorder, came into the country in 1897 and was a stinker, a grafter, a rake-off artist, and seduced Agate Alexander when she was only twelve years old. Says he would go out at night and unscrew the parts from heavy machinery that was passing through. Then when the people missed it in the morning, he'd say he happened to have such-and-such a spare part in his shed and sell it back to them. He loved to watch fights; loved to provoke fights by telling one that the other shouldn't be dumping mine tailings on his land and to do something about it, and then telling *him* that it was okay—"stand up for your rights." He had an asbestos showing on Germansen Creek which he called "petrified bananas," because of how asbestos looks. Luke Fowler used to stand up for Billy Steele and defend him,

and Luke cut wood for him, but when Luke wanted a cup
of coffee, Billy would give him the tin cup that he used for
a spittoon and gave him the dog's plate for a saucer. Luke
thought himself a little bit better than the other Indians
because of his Chinese blood, and he used to wash his feet
at night, but only his feet, because that was the part that
people had washed in the Bible.

Billy Martin had long black whiskers when he died,
down to his bellybutton, and no blood in him—you could
practically look through him. Skook Davidson, playing
bridge with a lady partner one day and not doing well,
said hold your cards next to your bellybutton and we'll
fuck them yet. Fred Aslin had eighteen kids, between his
two Indian wives. Harold Smith, a tough money-man,
used to sell the miners at Manson Creek maggoty bacon
which he couldn't sell to the Indians at Fort St. James; you
had to cut the rotten parts off. Tommy Perkins looked
like a white-haired judge, but was a bootlegger, and lived
in Art Hyndman's cabin. Frank Thompson took over Jack
Thompson's trapline and was always on the run, never
walked. He was up in his seventies when he disappeared
and died, and Nielsen doesn't figure that either the grizzlies or the Indians got him—he thinks it was heart failure. Frank Thompson bought war bonds, and dug so
many holes in the ground to hide them in that finally
even he couldn't find them. As for Bob Watson or Don
Gilliland, you "could write a chequebook" about either

one, he says. Gilliland has a crazy streak in his blood, was always cheating his neighbors or his hunting clients, or would elicit threatening letters and then send these to the police. He'd break into someone's cabin and, with a little hacksaw, would saw the snout off his kettle. And he shot regularly at the storekeepers across the Omineca from him. He called his wife "One-night Irene," before he married her. Then later people would ask him whether they could have her for their one-night stand. And the super-strong Bob Watson always had a pack on his back. "He was going no place, but he always had a pack on his back. I never seen anybody with a disease like that. Most of us pack only when we have to." The other great thing about Watson was that he got lost all the time. He'd wind up in Finlay Forks or at Takla Landing, when he'd just wanted to go to a neighbor's claim.

It's an awful thing what gold does to the soul, Nielson says. Mrs. Tait, a wonderful woman years ago, spent three quarters of a million dollars to take out what amounted to two thousand dollars in gold, and now she isn't so wonderful anymore. Her husband is a radiologist. Her brother was Billy Martin and he left her that strange diary about where to find gold when he died, which inspired all of this single-minded, expensive activity of hers. It's always been a rough country. Dagineau used to look at your hands before he'd even hire you—as if you were some kind of nigger—and half the mining outfits never paid their miners during the Hungry Thirties. (The others never paid their shareholders.) Neilson, though—when he quit—used to get about a salt shaker of gold dust out of them. Neilson used to wear socks and moccasins, and then heavy socks outside the moccasins for extra warmth. Once one of Agate Alexander's kids saw him in these outside socks and went home and told his mother, and she snowshoed up right away, four miles, to offer to make him a pair of snowshoes.

"That's when you find out what people are made of, when you need help," Nielson says. Agate's father came several miles up the Manson River with a small kicker on his dugout canoe to bring Neilson a chunk of moose meat afterward. Agate never slept with Johnny Nielson, but she told him to stay away from the young squaws, because "they're starting to smoke the white man," she said: in other words, suck, which means sliding downhill.

Joe Calper is another current resident. He's husky and has hair to his shoulders and a beard and walks into Neilson's cabin sometimes in the middle of the night and looks down at him in his bed. He ran away from his wife in Edmonton and went wild. When he's angry or crazy his hair and beard stand out straight, and his wife came up with a letter from a doctor to take him away, but he ran into the bush. Then she sent the cops, who came in an airplane to Manson Creek and caught him and took him to Prince George, but released him three weeks later.

Doc Bishop Thurber is another runaway here, a runaway geologist.

Johnny Neilson tells a burst of good-natured scandal like this for ten to fifteen seconds, then, cutting himself off, slides into an enigmatic hum. "Now I'm going to speak no more ill of my brother men," he says. He's very like Alex Rosen and Olaf Hogberg, two other Scandinavian bachelors. He says that he went up to Dagineau's mine one time to get a job, and the boss was shaving. He asked for a job, and the boss just glanced at him in the mirror and said no. Dagineau liked to do that. Most men had walked 140 miles, and he liked to make them beg and plead and then look at their hands and deliberate, and so on, before turning them down. But Johnny just said thank you and turned away and walked home.

JULY 8

Here I am, 180 miles from the nearest drugstore, with a fungus infection on my prick. And that's all the use it's being put to.

This is a lovely, unostentatious, hilly, tumbly country, with rolling, rotting flumes and trestles and loading platforms and gravel piles and rusted items of heavy machinery, and collapsed cabins, the wood weathered purple and red, everywhere. I came upon a lovely toad, green, black, and silver, very fat and warted, with lanky, enormous hind feet. This is civilized country—white man's country—with the housecats that everyone has. (These I'm allergic to, and also to insecticide; the day before yesterday I lay on my bed as if poisoned.) And many birdhouses for swallows are nailed atop poles. Wooden trays are set out with crumbled bread crumbs for the chipmunks and whisky jacks and assorted "peeper" birds, or the squirrels clinging onto the door screens like lizards. The animated trash truck, called Betsy, painted with figures, has a mirror that the bears and moose look in, too.

I talked to Ernie Floyd, who walked over the Wolverine Mountains from Finlay Forks (about forty-five miles) in 1932, which he later would regularly travel by dogsled. He says he camped one time with Skook Davidson when they'd met on the trail, and Skook told him his biggest regret in twenty years or so of wilderness living was that he'd had a loyal little dog and, once while camping one hungry winter night, the dog swiped his supper bacon, and he'd shot her in a fit of temper, and immediately wished like hell that he hadn't. "You've been alone too long, and you'll do that."

Charlie Farrell was a "wonderful underground man," Ernie said, and "a good timber man." He could put the tunnel timbers in to last. He drowned while snowshoeing on the Manson River. It was spring. The ice had wedged up under a covering of snow and the river had eaten a lot of it away from underneath; and his snowshoes broke through and he couldn't pull them out. Frank Johnson was a tall, slim guy who could really keep going, "a going hound," as Ernie Floyd puts it, a very hard worker. He was a lone operator and, sure, he took some mean shots at the Indians. But Floyd doesn't think he was killed by them, or by grizzlies, either. He'd worn very heavy glasses, so if he ever lost those glasses, he might have simply starved to death in that rough country, unable to find his way out. It was rugged and piled up with granite boulders, so one of those might have tumbled down on him, also. Or he might have fallen into a hole and broken a bone.

Roy Lord got mad at a parrot and threw a coat over him, covering him up. His parrot, panicking in the dark, then cried, "Where are you, Roy? Where are you, Roy?" Like Skook, with his little rabbit dog who was disobedient only once in her life, you get awfully close to an animal in this bush.

Ernie Floyd likes Don Gilliland and Harold Smith, and says you can kid them along if they're feeling stubborn. He also liked Billy Steele, whom he says was liberal with his information, especially to greenhorns, as long as you didn't rub him the wrong way. He was more of a placer than a hardrock miner, and therefore secretive, because placer miners need to be secretive because their paydirt is so near the surface. Floyd has three groups of claims right at the moment, each with a different partner: a scheelite (tungsten) claim on lower Lost Creek, a columbite claim (alloy of steel) on lower Granite Creek, and a molybdenum claim on Mill Creek. He says when he first came into the country, he counted twenty-one foundations of the original cabins, but that Hudson's Bay had stupidly bulldozed them flat. He lives in a cluttered old cookhouse, dating from the 1930s, with a bumpy hewed floor, the planks all broadaxe work, and two centrepoles that he's recently put in to hold the roof up, and a stove that came all the way from Quebec. Has a sly, clear, clean, little, humorous face, like Walter Lippman's; blue eyes; looks upward a lot. A neat, slight body. An odd combination of pictures are stuck on the wall—sentimental Norman Rockwell, alongside the rawest harem of pinups.

I went to the Manson Creek cemetery. The rude crosses on the handful of graves are marked with each name and the date of death simply written by lines of nail-heads that were pounded into the wood. As well as the bickering and feuding, there is a lot of straight cursing among the citizens here, which you don't have in older towns, like Hazelton and Telegraph Creek, or in the real Indian towns either. Not that the Indians are content or "pure-minded"; but they're no longer really at home in their own languages, and not so much in the white man's either. So they may talk a bit awkwardly, as if walking in ill-fitting shoes.

I've been sleeping in so many different beds that I have no sense of direction when I wake up in the night (as I do, abruptly).

JULY 9

We get water from the creek down a fifty-foot drop by means of a marvellous drag line, which we wind on a drum.

Why is it precious to me that my loved one has certain ears—I think of Marion's ears in baby-talk terms—when everyone else whom I see also has ears, and I don't give a damn? Love seems to key our humanity to a pitch.

We in the city deprive ourselves of air, light, space, and green and blue vistas, a deprivation of such magnitude one can hardly think what could be worse. But people here are denied the delights of good food, and the pleasurable soaking of a hot bath, and much conversation, and news of the world, and, above all, the softnesses and amplitude of women—women in the plural, at least, even if they have a wife. I think if I had to choose one place irrevocably, I might choose to live here, but since I don't have to, I live primarily in New York.

As I've said, it's tricky to compare the Indian-white situation in British Columbia with the Negro-white set-up in the US. In the sense that a genuine intimacy or amity does exist and the discrimination is not brutally oppressive, it might resemble Virginia or North Carolina. Nearly all the older people have memories of friendship (or love life) with individual Indians, but they want to see them treated more roughly than the government does—a sort of perpetual Hungry Thirties for them, on minimal Welfare. The younger group doesn't want to see them so roughly used, as a rule, because *they* haven't gone hungry and hoofed it for miles, and so can't imagine anybody having to. But they haven't the fond memories of them, individually, either. Their relative liberalism is cold in its tone, like the North's towards the blacks. (I should mention I was at Martin Luther King's March on Washington five years ago.)

In the highway era to come, of course, we will drive from one town to another, and it will be a matter of minutes and miles. At present, in the bush-plane era, the terminology and the destinations are always stated as *lakes,* even when you are driving along a dirt bush track to get there: not flying and then landing on pontoons. Before, in the era of hiking and horse-packing, destinations, locations, and geography were generally given as *rivers* and *creeks.* These were the valleys, the homesites, the sources of larder (or obstacles).

Today Bruce Russell, the freighter, and I spent twelve hours going up Uslika from Manson Creek again, fifty miles or so, and back, the road is so bad. We saw ravens, and reddish ground squirrels, and baby grouse running and flying up, and two black young bull moose, who looked like donkeys from the rear as they ran away on their stick legs. It reminds me of the gold country elsewhere, in the Cassiar and Cariboo ranges: no spectacular, rugged peaks, but a rolling, chopped-up, creeky, conifer country, averaging three thousand feet, with moderate rainfall, where sedimentary gold had been trapped. He pointed out an old flume, set against the face of a sand cliff, which he'd used to haul lumber for, a total of nine miles of ditch-and-flume, he said. Rain turns the Omineca River molten like metal—the valley is full of rain like cotton batting. There is snow falling in the north country today, so we wondered whether Sam and George had gotten safely across the Mesilinka, which is a faster river, with more fall to it, until the winter will put the lid on again. Already rose petals are starting to fall. By August 15, the leaves will be turning yellow. Uslika Lake (a surveyor's joke name?) was ruffled with rain and breezes, and then still again, reflecting the chunky blue mountains to the south, or grey, green, and tawny, with majestically coloured reflections from the sidehills and the trees like hieroglyphics in a vastly rich carpet. A campful of contract prospectors were there—lanky guys lifted in from Vancouver, bitter and harsh and cursing, telling the barren, dead-end jokes which men without women tell, though of course they were having some fun too. A convoy of five American tourist families had managed to reach the lake by dirt road, and had huddled their tents together at the far end of the water, as if they were in Indian country. They were not happy, and the Canadians were enjoying their discomfiture. The water in the Osilinka is still too high for fly-fishing to be any good: too muddy for the fish to see well, and also too full of natural fish food. In fact, it won't be much good until just about the time when the ice starts to skin over and stopper it all over again.

We picked up Sam's bearpaw snowshoes, which he'd left for storage (must be put where the pack rats can't get at them). They say he and George had a bit of a rodeo going before they could start—the horses bucked off their stuff. Since they've left, a whole new bunch of horses have come in for the hunting season, a whole string that is infected with a throat virus—horse pills everywhere. Bruce had any number of errands to do in Germansen Landing. The Gillilands are installing a radio phone, so they needed to have the use of it explained to them. It was great, explaining the use of a phone. And Santa Claus Joe Calper had ordered in a new stove. And a placer prospector had wanted a female-fitting to attach to his acetylene tank, instead of the male one he had. Driving through a twenty-mile burn, I noticed areas which were only scorched, where the fire had just crawled along. The ground was ashen-white and so were the trunks of the trees, but not the treetops. The treetops were green. Whether it's false or not, there's a sense in this country of contact with ultimates, as though all the world's sources and secrets might be around the next bend.

JULY 10

The Bertrand Russell *Autobiography* is remarkably incomplete. Of course a good part of it consists of letters to him from other people, who neither write well nor say very much. Russell's own account has an admirable frankness, but even this is defeated sometimes by his brevity and by all he leaves out, not so much for reasons of reticence as for want of trying. We know, for instance, how passionate he was in certain climactic moments, but not the roots of the passion or really what the results finally were, in terms of suffering, or regrets afterward, or indecisive floundering. What little he's written is generous-spirited enough and engrossing and often imbued with the visionary genius, but there's just so sadly little! Why he thought the project of writing an autobiography wasn't worth a solid effort I can't understand. (Six years ago, in Vence, France, I knew one of his lovers, the radiant Hungarian beauty, Countess Károlyi.)

Santa Claus Joe Calper just walked by. He *looks* like the greatest old-timer of all, with his white beard and bear's build, but he's actually a newcomer and a cipher. Doc Bishop Thurber interests me more, the homey, bashful, runaway geologist, deep-voiced and unkempt, with white stubble whiskers, doggy eyebrows, and a dirty grey shirt. He looks like Pluto, the dog in the old Mickey Mouse comic books, and has named his own dog Viking. He was up here on surveys as early as 1937 and has come back at troubled times ever since. Is obviously a woman-oriented fellow; probably with much marital trouble. Has an inferiority complex and a sulphurous, lava-like cough, an incredibly convoluted and serious cough. What he does best is walk. He lives with Johnny Nielsen, who runs a kind of boarding house for the prospectors who pass through; busily cooks their steaks and gossips with them. Doc talks with lots of parenthetical, swallowed yeps, like a man who mostly talks to himself. He says he was seventeen when he left Copenhagen, came to the States illegally, and worked twenty-seven months on a sea-going lumber tug before pushing west. The biggest adventure was once when the tug was run down by a tanker. He found himself swimming and thought the world was coming to an end and saw his suitcases floating away. In Hoboken, New Jersey, where they tied up, it was so tough that their watchman was murdered one night, and the boat robbed. He says that the bush is the safest place to be. You quarrel with a partner once in a while, because he hangs the frypan on the wrong nail, and maybe you have one or two dangerous experiences with the wildlife in thirty years. But, in the city, you've got those cars and those bicycles coming at you all the time. He had a scary experience thirty miles out from here one time, though it happened so fast that he wasn't scared until later on. He saw what he thought was a moose calf lying down across the path ahead of him; and that at least got him alert. When he arrived at the place, something like twenty wolves dashed out of ambush from both sides, half of them yellow, and half of them grey. He swung his pack off his back and threw it in front of him, got his axe in his hands, and gave a big yell, and they ran. They had thought *he* was the mother moose. He'll shake and shiver, telling a joke, and then sit very still.

Johnny Nielsen wears slippers, customarily, and his ashtrays are shaped like toilets, studded with glass jewels. He has a "Bullshit" eye chart on the wall. The packboard nailed outside his cabin door is a symbol of what he did— how he lived—however, trekking to every stream, looking originally for nuggets, and then for the motherlode gold.

I walked three to four miles down a side road and found George Ikas, an isolated little man, happy in his work, as they say. He's diminutive and precise, like a jockey, with a ladylike voice, a resigned, wrinkled-up, round, bony, whimsical face, with flat cheeks, big ears, a firm chin, and clear eyes—a friendly, underfed, humble-natured sort of man, who wears high wool socks and garters for them, and suspenders for his heavy pants, and has one thickened finger stub; otherwise is uninjured. After the Depression, he came in from the Cariboo and Chilcotin country, his prospecting partner a former pool-room proprietor. They were both broke and adventuring. They "sniped" a few miles south of Manson Creek for loose flakes of gold, and worked on the claim of an old fellow they met who was kind enough to let them keep whatever they found. George then worked for several of the hydraulic-equipped companies who dredge deeper under streambeds for gold, as well as on the highway, and in logging camps. In World

War II, he was in "Continental Europe" with the Canadian army, he says, but came back and eventually built a spare, bare cabin out of old mining-flume boards, and a plywood interior, and staked one of the claims which he'd previously worked for a salary, and which the company had let lapse. He's cleared a stark little yard, and girdled a stand of pine trees for firewood.

George Ikas offers me the inevitable cup of coffee, which people live on here, and sets out a gold pan full of cookies and biscuits. It's a cheap way of living for an old man, he says: not too much work, and just the claim lease to pay, by way of rent. Tiny and even fragile though he looks, he has indefatigable nervous energy. He tells me that he never bothered with trapping furs—he likes the wild animals too much—though he knows you can't even make proper wages at placer-mining any more. But it's a free life. You have the summer to yourself, the long daylight hours, and your own cabin and grub. Unless you get out and prospect on contract or a salary for the base metals (which no one wanted before World War II) or hunt gemstones and polishing-rocks such as jade, it's just a hobby. You'll find a few nuggets to sell to the jeweller, and a few ounces of gold grains to send to the Royal Canadian Mint to smelt. And good fishing. There's lake trout, dollies, rainbows, and char. He's got a new second-hand stove that cost thirty dollars, with his box of powdered Carnation Mashed Potatoes sitting on top. His claim lies on Government Creek, and, as a labour of love, he constructed a lovely flume that runs in a clover-leaf—had a one-ton hand winch at the sluice for hauling up rock. Though there is pockety gold sign left—two or three ounces here or there, or some colour in some of the sand—the gold is pretty well beat out of his creek, it's been so heavily worked. Yet he wants to do a little more ditching and fluming here, and scrape up an old dry stream bed nearby. Then in August, he usually goes out prospecting with Ernie Floyd, after the first frosts have killed the mosquitoes and they just have the black flies to contend with. They find "mineral occurrences," like hobbyists, but don't entertain any hopes any longer of a big grand-slam ore body which the "heliflapters" may have missed. He's been fluming water to an old pit he dug, but the water source is about played out now. Instead, as another labour of love, he's built a fantastic long footbridge (186 feet!) over the creek, complete with approaches and cable railings. Shy and self-effacing, he wishes me gone, except when we get out to see these works and workings. There, he's relaxed and proud, not in a hurry.

It was a splendid walk back. I saw bluebells, fool grouse, and moose tracks. The poplar forests were white in the sun. Then the sky filled up with yellow clouds, a mustard colour, and a sudden hard rain. Abruptly, the forest was flooded, with the white lichen and green moss thankful for it. There was a double-rainbow, very close to me and bright—a garish green and a marmalade orange—which plunged into the earth right on this side of the nearest hill. But in fifteen minutes it all cleared away to a cloudless, brilliant, pale blue.

Beef stew for supper (salmon loaf yesterday), and baking-powder biscuits with huckleberry jelly, and chocolatized milk. In reading frontier accounts of journeys and jaunts, one is struck by the number of people who die. My "morning cough," which develops so fast, as soon as I leave town life, assures me that I could be one of them. The madness too. More fantasies: a slave boy who must fix his eyes on his mistress's bust and keep them there as long as she wishes.

A strange California family lives here: a lonely, "eyeless" little boy; pretty, uneducated girls; a soft-hearted wife, who is shaped like a bear and walks like a man; and a substanceless, rootless husband, soft and suburban in mind, but athletic in body and build.

I'd stopped to see Ernie Floyd again, in returning from George Ikas's bridge. He heated coffee for me on the Coleman stove, which saves time, compared to lighting the wood stove. He said a friend of his scalded his leg with boiling coffee water one time, but jumped in the creek—"a good treatment, you know." Everyone here lives on coffee. No food seems to be eaten at breakfast or lunch; no food is apparent in the cabins. Everybody is spry and thin and limber. He has a long-barrelled .22 for shooting "chickens" (grouse) in the woods, and an old Winchester lever-action .30 Navy rifle for moose, though it's really too heavy to pack very far. He has a duck-billed wood stove, and several wooden chests, and stacks of cardboard boxes everywhere, and trinkets and curios hanging up; also a rat trap. He says when a mother pack rat runs, she gets her young ones to hang on for dear life to her nipples and they swing under her. He kills these furry-tailed rats, but doesn't kill any game in the summer, a time when you'd only get one or two feeds anyway from the creature before the meat rotted, and he likes having the animals around, doesn't like shooting them. He was out this morning. Being July now, the country is getting pretty badly brushed up; it's hard work, walking. It was kind of warm, but by golly a little wind blew up—makes a big difference when you're hiking—and better than a rain, because wet brush will tear the pants right off of you. He stays off the blazed trails because he wants to see the new country empty, not looked-at, and now most of these cabins "have running water," he says. He likes to lie under the stars and count them, instead of counting sheep. He carries a powerful magnifying glass to look at mineral specimens, and has key rings and regular rings "made up" from gemstones he finds. He's a small, cat-like man with a high smooth voice, feminine in a way, like so many of these old bachelors who have cooked and mended for themselves all these years, and has clear eyes like a blue flame—a man of plentiful curiosities and a tinkering nature. He's even found dinosaur bones in the coal beds around. For the winter he goes out to Lillooet, but gets way up in the hills there too. It's rather hopeless, though—always waiting for some big company to mosey along and take your discovery off your hands.

When he first came into Stewart, near the coast, in the stiff mountain range where Alaska meets Canada, about eighty old-timers were living there, and they'd put a big welcome sign on the dock: "No Orientals Wanted Here." Then the country emptied, when the surface gold was exhausted. They'd just left the wolves and the caribou to fight it out, under the ice fields. The entrance to his own mine tunnel looked like a root cellar, next to his cabin, and he always told people that's what it was, when they stopped by, so they'd never know where his tunnel was located. But you get discouraged and move along.

JULY 11 AND 12

Art Hyndman is the senior old-timer in Manson Creek, now that Bob Watson has died. The position carries with it a certain esteem, and he's a wry, dry, sizable fellow, wearing glasses with two-colour frames. He has a creaky voice, a mild, small-town manner—not the tough man-of-the-bush—and hasn't a very good memory for the stories he tells, but chuckles to himself a lot. He's bald, and perches gracefully on his bunk, which is set up on stacked sluice boxes, while he's talking. The ceiling of the log cabin is low, and blackened from the smoking stove. There's a relic couch, a number of broken chairs standing about as stools, a board floor, and lots of clocks around, wound and unwound, a Coleman stove for cooking, a 1957 calendar posted up, a 1960 calendar, and a 1967 calendar; heaps of reading material, such as an 1870 "Commercial Mathematics" text, and clothes hung all over the walls from nails, mostly pants, and towels, plus boots all over the floor.

Hyndman came to Canada from the north of Ireland in 1912. Ten years later he reached the Ingenika River from Fort Grahame on the Finlay, and then lived at Germansen Lake. The first white settlement in the area had been built around Discovery Bar, on the Omineca, Art says. Three graves there, dated 1872, give New York State, Kentucky, and Berkshire, England, as birthplaces. It was abandoned at the time of the Cassiar rush, a good deal northward of here. The second town was at the Kildare Gulch strike; and then the whole area, by the twenties, when he arrived, had been abandoned again. The closest store then was over at Takla Landing. A bunch of people walked in to try yet again during the Depression, however, and Hudson's Bay built its Manson Creek store. Archie King, Ralph Meissener, and he were the youngsters, and Billy Steele and Luke Fowler were the old-timers. Archie King had been a second mate in the British merchant marine. He worked a donkey engine at the Kildare Creek findings.

But Luke Fowler travelled alone, and placer-mined alone, and hard, "more like a Chinaman than an Indian." Luke liked to use long words like "observation"; and he always was wrong on the weather, but liked to tell you his predictions anyway. He finally worked on Blackjack Creek, when a company brought in some hydraulic machinery, and came back to snipe nuggets there the rest of his life, after they had abandoned it.

Frank Johnson was tall and long-legged, "quite a going concern," as Art puts it. "Would take double the length of the steps of an average man," and a crack shot with a pistol. He left his cabin as if maybe he had suddenly just run out—with stew still on the stove, and books on the bench outside the door. Maybe he got caught in his own bear trap. He liked to set those. There was an awful fall of wet snow at that time, so if he hurt himself and was pinned, it would have been hard to get a fire going. They should have watched the whisky jacks and the fox tracks, if they wanted to find his body, Art suggests. That's how you do it. Ed Moore and his partner were old Yukoners, coming down the Telegraph Trail and then east towards here, when they got into trouble. The partner may simply have gone through the Sustut ice. A guy named McLaren and his partner also disappeared in that Bear Lake country, which made people suspicious of the Indians. Some of the Bear Laker band had black whiskers, as if a Frenchman might have gotten in among them. Every once in a while, when they got rowdy, the police would go in and straighten them out.

Nat Porter had once been a boxer in the US, Art says. Cap Hood was "an awful size of a man," a military police-man during World War 1. Fred Aslin had had two stores, in fact, one of which he gave to his wife when they sepa-rated. He had tramped in during the Depression originally, sniping, like so many did. Billy Steele, with Jack Mull-ins, worked on Lost Creek—"pretty sly, pretty bad, quite a twister." Hyndman chuckles, when he mentions Billy. "He was a terror when he had a few drinks in him. Poured hot mush down a fellow's throat on the Skeena. Knocked another guy out with a club on the Omineca." Skook was another toughie: a Highland Scotsman. Drinking over-proof rum with Frank Cooke in a contest one time, he got so red that finally he lost and fell on the floor. Ed Sullivan carried a big axe—as big as himself—and was threaten-ing to chop you up with it. He had brought in a donkey engine over heavy snow, and he "went out to Burns Lake and died there. He was pretty old." Poor guy had jack-hammered for years and years through hard rock to get to an old river channel. "Well, when he got to it, he had turned at right-angles too high, you know, so he had to start over."

Harold Smith was "quite a rustler, quite a peddler." Such a liar: a "big handshake and a big smile, and he'd cut your throat if he got the chance." Charlie Farrell was an old coal miner, now after gold. "Come in," he'd say. "I'm tired of talking to myself, and I'm not liking the answers I'm getting, either." He went through a hole in the ice on Manson Creek, when he was on his way into town to fix his lease papers, and never climbed out. Bob Watson and Erickson, both over seventy, had a fist fight outdoors, blood flying, over who could lift a big drum of gas. Watson couldn't fight well when he was drunk, and Erickson hollered so loud anyway you would think a fight was going on all the time. He had been a blacksmith in the Swedish army and had been taught to holler loud. Ralph Meissener came in in 1923 with some horses, and worked on some diggings of Billy Steele's. Lost the horses during his second winter. No feed. Was from Nova Scotia, and quite a worker; used a water wheel in place of a turbine engine for his power to lift the gravel out of the diggings. And no matter where he was, he always grew flowers. Tough old guy, though. Somebody once tied a horse to his fence, and the horse pulled down the fence and ate the flowers, and it made for a lifetime's quarrel.

Art Hyndman has Johnny Nielsen's taste for gossip and scandal, but seldom will repeat what he's chuckling at. The more stories he can think of in regard to somebody, the fewer he tells me; the sheer number and variety seem to discourage him. Hamburger Joe operated a boat on the Parsnip River for the Forestry Service, he says, after giving up prospecting. Mort Tier and Ben Cork died in the hospital, after being brought off the Finlay. Jake Fries died of appendicitis on this river. Gene Marie—who was the boss of the small band of Indians on the Omineca, along with Agate—had the long Sikanni nose of the Interior Indians, whereas "these Carriers look like a Chinaman or a Jap."

"Hello, King George, Man!" Gene Marie would say, talking to a big shot. He did the step dance, and played "The Irish Washerwoman" on his fiddle—"Good Indian, but also a blowhard who beat his chest." He used to bring the priest over from Takla Landing by dogsled, and once, when the priest put his false teeth in a cup of water for the night, they froze there, and in the morning, when he tried to chip them loose, the priest broke the plate. "That's the first time I ever heard the father swear," says Art. Pierre John, who was married to Stazzy Marie, was a better Indian, he says. But most of the Indians "would bum you to death if they could. Always short of sugar"—a cup of their tea was half full of sugar. "Long time since I see you. Pretty near I cry. You got a little sugar?" They used sugar and raisins and rice or cornmeal for homebrew. Art wears a half-smile as he speaks of the Indians: An Indian doesn't travel fast but he travels a long way, stopping to make tea whenever he's tired.

Art's most recent adventure was when a bear tried to climb into his cabin. He had knocked the stovepipe down and the radio over, pushing his big head through the window, but when Hyndman started yelling, he pulled out. At first when he heard the bear's thumping, he dreamed he was still down in the hotel at the Fort and that they were moving packing boxes.

"A big bear, but a couple of hundred pounds shy of winter. I don't know what was wrong with him. It was October, and he was thin and probably thought he couldn't get through the winter without more to eat, or maybe he'd got some wolf poison in him. He'd found some strawberry jam by the sink, anyway, so he tramped around leaving red traces." Art thought he must have cut himself on the window. They finally poisoned him, and then when they heard him roaring in pain in the bush, they went up and shot him to save him some misery.

I talked until late last night with a renegade intellectual from Indiana, extremely good company, Peter Dickerson. Add him to Santa Claus Joe Calper, who has recently fled his wife, and to the junior-high principal from California, who has an ulcer and owns this general store, and to the two moustachioed young jade hunters who live across the creek, as signs of the times. He told me how he heard the wolf packs singing last winter, after two kills. It was also their mating season, so the ululation, like a mouth organ, or like the celebrative honking of a chorus of horns, was from a combination of emotions. Afterwards, only the frozen stomach contents of the moose were left, and parts of the bony heads and pieces of hide. One moose had been killed where he stood, browsing on willows and, from the tracks, seemed to have put up little fight. Mostly we talked of the exhilarating vaguenesses that intellectuals like to make reference to once every month or so, death and life. But, as a matter of business, I got him to tell me about his mauling by a grizzly bear, too, off the Alcan Highway, last summer. He was very calm in his description or attitude, except that he swallowed a lot and rubbed his head where his scars are, and spoke sadly and finally with agitation, though he says that he never dreams about, never relives, it in a nightmare. It's made him super-alert and rather intimidated in the woods.

He says the incident was as sudden, stunning, and quick as being hit by a car. He was descending a rough, rock-studded hill, with the noise of a stream covering the sounds that he made. Then, down in the hollow, watching mostly his footing, he started up the other side, which was topped by a thicket of brush. He looked up and suddenly the grizzly was coming down at him like a runaway car, absolutely terrifying. It had been eating a fetid moose that a hunter had killed, and he stumbled and fell on his back and drew his feet up over him instinctively as a shield. The bear—which the tracks afterward showed to be large— did not attempt to bite him, and it ignored his feet and legs, though they were his only defence. It swatted him three or four times. The first was the hardest. This blow hit him next to the eye, causing a popping sound and making him think he had lost it. The bear's breath was perhaps worst of all, "like a dragon's breath." He didn't play dead or employ any of the other recommended techniques, but it moved away, acting "beside itself" and as if "torn by" conflicting impulses—a fear as great as his was, and a horror of him, as well as its rage at being interrupted on the moose, and its predatory pride. He thinks each of them was equally appalled and scared. But then it came back and hit him again. He says its claws were as sharp as knives, ripping his clothes, his wallet inside his clothes, and even his money inside his wallet, before, fortunately, its anger was appeased.

As for his thinking, Peter is self-educated and seems widely, if obscurely, read in philosophy and historicism. He longs for a unified, circumscribed world, like mediaeval society, and thinks he is here in the Canadian woods to stay. In fact, he wants to buy somebody's trapline. He's German-oriented in the literature and philosophy he admires; has spent a year away from his wife, and now thinks that he wants her to join him—the problem of mail between them last winter was so terrible. He's a clear-faced, red-faced man in his forties, strongly built, and apparently self-contained. His very critical ideas of modern life and modern America (though I could begin to agree) seemed to me overly alarmist, exaggerated, and one-sidedly informed, but he's by no means a nut. He says, incidentally, that his snowshoe trips in the woods have no relation to his regimen of reading and writing—no rhythmic or oppositional or balancing or complementary relationship.

I RETURNED from Manson Creek to Fort St. James with young Larry Erickson, the ablest current hunting guide in this section of British Columbia. He's personable, enlightened, and educated with regard to game habits and habitat, has worked for biologists, trained falcons, and run sled dogs. We stopped to smell wild orchids and roses and pick lupine and paintbrush. Once we had to stop nearly for good because a beaver dam had broken and inundated the road for two hundred yards with floods of water two feet deep. We talked about the phenomenon of "cabin fever," which afflicts isolated partners and turns them cranky, and about how these cold rainy springs sometimes kill off the year's crop of baby grouse with pneumonia. His favourite weeks are those he spends in the summer out alone with his huskies, hiking. The three of them can carry up to sixty pounds, each, and like wolves, need to be stuffed with groundhogs, whole, once every three or four days, but not fed otherwise. He says the grizzlies are doing well on all the moose that people shoot. He's also pro-wolf. He tells me that Gilliland's wife was a prostitute before her marriage, and that Larry Owens, when he taught school down in the Fort last year, lived with a pretty blonde teacher and kept his family up at Manson Creek, with all the snows separating them. It's necessary to have a few gleeful informants like him and Nielsen and Hogberg to balance the solid-citizen types who let no ill word escape them. He reminds me that the incoming trappers used to stop at a post like Fort Ware in the fall and pick up a squaw, as well as their winter's grubstake.

Fort St. James, again: and the high-shouldered silhouettes of the Indian men, as if they had on a perpetual pack. And an Indian girl as big as a man but rounder and jouncier, with brown swinging hair, a soft face, and large lips that seldom manage to close. She'd be my pick.

Alex Leggatt, an intense, fast-moving, businesslike fellow, is fairly deaf, so our renewed conversation for a while is a comedy of misunderstandings. His old partner, Alex Rosen, is blind in one eye and always keeps that side turned away. John Prince, sitting in a suit of long underwear, reading, says, laughing, "Today's Saturday, a holiday," when I ask for some stories. "So, no stories till five o'clock." Then, of course, by five he's left. I went to the movie at the gymnasium, instead. It was supposed to be *The Killers,* but wasn't. Cold metal chairs, not an adult in the house. Boys stoning dogs outside. They whimper as the stone is thrown, but don't wait for it to be thrown. This fantastic view of the lake we're on; all day and night is never dark. The best of me, I sometimes think, is this jumping in and out of trucks, hauling my duffel bag with me, and hiking up to a ramshackle old-timer's cabin.

JULY 14

Sunday. I've been resting, bathing, eating three meals a day, all highly unusual occupations, and getting my bowels back in shape. As I've said, this rough living doesn't come easily to me, and I get worn out both physically and emotionally by all this exhausting stuttering to strangers besides. I've been reading *A Moveable Feast,* which is really rather a pale rerun of Hemingway's earlier stuff, but he was so very good that it's good.

I talked to Rosen again. He's more affectionate and effusive every time he sees me. His masklike, mutilated face bobs in mock-solemnity and he yodels. He does a solo, bravura performance for me on the question of the soul. What is it? The doctors when they "disseminate" a corpse don't find anything, do they? Is it a gas? He doesn't kneel down to anybody or anything. He's happy just to be out in the open, letting the squirrels chirp their theology at him. "Well, you won't live long," he says back to them. But gold exerts some kind of fascination for people, he tells me. You get some in an empty medicine bottle and shake it in front of them—grains and flakes—and the people that see it, they go wild! It's like lure to a fish. You throw it to some poor yokel that's come off of the farm, and he goes crazy. He'd buy anything you want to sell him. A hundred yards of a brook. Or the old guys—like a colony of prairie dogs—they'll pop their heads out of the creek as you walk by—the miners—like a colony of animals, with their nattering bickering.

I went to see John Prince again for some stories, since he'd stood me up yesterday. But because it is Sunday, he has led the prayers at three services already and is sleepy, and still breakfastless, so old that I feel guilty every time he leans forward to hear what I'm trying to say, or stands up to get me a picture. (Jimmy Alexander, in a suit and tie, for instance, tall, leader-like, moustached, intelligent, and "Mediterranean" in appearance, instead of "Indian.") John suffers from arthritis in his shoulders. They've clenched his arms up almost double and he tries to flex the pain out of them continually. His nose is flattened-looking; his mouth a hole surrounded by wrinkles. The cabin smells rancid. It's hung with half a dozen saws and several canes and a portrait of himself in a tuxedo in Quesnel, circa 1906, for his wedding. There's a throne-like chair against one log wall, but the stove is a converted barrel. A pump from a well hangs over the sink, and electrical wiring hangs in loops along other walls. He has his white shirt and black necktie on for church, and asks me what stories I want to hear, while rain makes a popping sound on the roof, although the sun is still shining. He says he carried the mail from here to Finlay Forks and packed some grub for the miners enroute. Hudson's Bay gave him some money to buy furs in the wintertime, too.

"The Indian good people, then. If Indian go after girl, the chief and watchman tie him up and he have to kneel and do penance; then let him go. No white man then except Hudson's Bay and priest. Now, lots of white men, white man's school, and Indians crazy, Indians steal, fight all the time, get drunk. Half "free-married" now. Long time ago, nobody free-married, all married by the church." And he laughs, recalling how nobody believed that the railroad would ever come through: "Lots of windfall, lots of river—how railroad going to come through, how they going to get across? Now all these people getting high-tone because they all work hard, have money, but in those days they have no money, just slip of paper from the Hudson Bay for what furs they turned in." On the Fraser River he worked for a dollar twenty-five a day, lining the steamboat along the bank. "Good rum—better rum than now—cost that," he says.

He guided rich men too; he's the Indian they wanted guiding them. "Sometimes they too sick to go out after caribou, although they come all that way to hunt. One time saw forty-seven caribou but rich man was too sick to follow them; don't get *one*. They good shots, though. I throw stone up and two brothers hit it every time. Even Herbert Hoover came to Fort St. James. He seem scared; he shivering; scared of Indians, maybe, you know." John Prince was the one who made him sit down. "And then one Indian put hat on him, one put moccasins, another come and put moosehide pants on him, and one put moosehide coat on him." W.B. Fraser himself was there, officiating—descended from Simon Fraser, the explorer for whom British Columbia's great river is named.

"You make a book and send me one before I die," John Prince says to me. He tells about the sturgeons that were nine and a half feet long, with a head that alone weighed sixty pounds. "I like 'em," he says, smiling. "No bones at all. Used to run up the rivers before the mining screwed them up." He says liquor is "white man's water." He says before the white man came in such numbers, every Indian family had two or three cows, a team of horses, and a big plowed field behind the house. "Now if one Indian is drunk in the beer parlour they kick him out, but if a white man is drunk they don't kick him out. So Indian goes out in the bush and drinks bad stuff—drinks snuff and beer and vanilla extract, mixed—and that makes his heart start to wiggle and stop."

In the old days, he says, a silver fox skin was the most valuable, but the common trading item was the beaver skins. One skin was worth a fifty-pound sack of flour. Three skins bought a hat, five skins brought good boots. But there were bad traders, too, at the posts, and nobody else to go to, who'd give out a tin cupful of tea leaves for a single skin, and put their thumb inside the cup while they were measuring it. There was no paper sack to pour it in, so you tied up your purchase in your handkerchief. But the Indians kicked about that. One hundred pounds of sugar came in a square box, and the trader doled it out in exchange for furs. The trader would give the Indian chief a sack of black gunpowder and a sack of lead bullets to procure a whole winter's supply of rabbits for the band. You'd catch spawning salmon too, to dry and then freeze for the winter. But you'd go into that trader with a good rabbit skin and he'd never bother to say how much it was worth. As quick as he could, he'd throw it under the counter, before anybody had had any chance to look at it, and cut off a little plug of tobacco and put that down in its place for you.

JULY 15

In Prince George (almost a little city), I called up Hugo Stahlberg, who lives here, and asked him: "Were you shot by Bear Lake Charlie?" And he said yes, but wouldn't go into it. The other thing that I did in Prince George was eat in the same Chinese restaurant where Amy and I ate in 1960, on our honeymoon. It's good. The library, though, is like a store. People come "shopping" in it and talk at full voice. People say they make nine hundred dollars a month falling timber, and more in the mines.

The immigrant cook in the hotel kitchen has Europe still stamped on his face—big features sticking out, and a baggy suit; a buxom German wife, like the old-time hurdy-gurdy tent-show girls. I called up a guy named Ted Williams I'd heard about, with a voice like the Lone Ranger, who spoke well of Shorty Webber—a reputed murderer and thief—but said that a man named Scott on the Parsnip River—supposedly already wanted elsewhere, when he came into the country—was rumoured to have killed two men. They left notes saying that, if they disappeared, it would have been him. And it was an Indian from John Prince's family, of Fort St. James, who shot the two German boys on Olsen Creek, on the Finlay—Messner and Pfeiffer, a former upholsterer and a painter in oils, who had come to hunt gold—who were left to die on the ice. He was mentally off, he says, a bit of a simpleton. The Prince family (these Indian surnames were borrowed from eclectic sources) then disowned him.

Am reading *Newsweek* again. The new cruel world of assassinations is not a world I want to be famous in. In any case, I doubt that I ever will be a famous writer now, but don't crave fame as I used to in the fifties.

JULY 17

Today I flew to Watson Lake, in the Yukon, in hopes of seeing Skook Davidson, the last of the celebrated old-timers, who is still living the old life, on the Kechika, or "Big Muddy," River. It was a commercial flight, but proceeded by homey stages, the plane refueling at every town, like a bush plane, and everybody climbing out to stroll in the sun and visit the washroom, as if we were on a Greyhound bus and this were a rest stop. At Fort St. John, the Avis Rent a Car "girl" was near forty and had her small child behind the counter spending the day with her. Hertz was represented by a gentle old codger who looked in his sixties and wore no tie, although his shirt was buttoned right up to the collar. The country alongside the Alcan Highway is unspectacular, but sometimes the hills from the air seem terraced like a Mediterranean scene because of the parallel cutting the rivers have done. And the present valleys are complicated by isolated oxbows or bends the rivers have left by a turn. Then there's the incredible swiftness of the passing clouds, almost like motorcyclists.

After the many things I've heard about Skook, I await our meeting with some trepidation. On the one hand, he's "a hard old man whose stories will curl your hair," and, on the other, a gentle, debilitated fellow who has an Indian boy there cutting firewood for him, while he drives the team of horses to collect it. His voice on the radio, here at Stan Bridenti's Watson Lake air station—which is his contact point—sounds thoroughly vigorous. The privations of being alone, though, have just about worn me out. I'm feeling vulnerable and consumed, and have had enough. Then, the vast, benign summer night comes on, however, as bright as day in the North, and balmy and blue. The light isn't punishing, as it would be in Texas, only bright. I sat after supper watching a sliding-eyed, lanky waitress of, I suppose, nineteen—too young to live by herself—while reading Updike's appropriate story, "The Bulgarian Poetess." She's only the second girl I've fallen for, in all this long time, not because I'm impervious, but because most of the girls up here in the wide blue yonder seem so graceless.

The two thousand-mile Alaska Highway depresses me, once again, with its blasts and funnels of dust, the eternally blackened cars, the dynamite trucks, the trailers hauling huge orange bridge girders, each as long as a railroad car, and tuckered-out carloads of Marylanders. It's remarkable: the gruesome resemblance between members of the same family.

I looked up Hans Anderson—from my first visit, two years ago. His nose is even more startlingly hooked than I remembered. He's shy and mild-mannered, however, and owns a whole cluster of shacks and very old trucks or derelict, bullet-shaped trailers, set up on blocks, to rent as housing; also the building the grocery store occupies, which has a totem pole lying on the ground in back, amidst all of the firewood. He says they accumulate up to eight feet of snow by January; it just about covers the roofs. I asked if there wasn't some trapper in town I should talk to. He said he didn't know.

"How about your tenant there?" I pointed towards an old fellow he rents to.

"Oh, him. He's the oldest trapper in the whole country, I think. He's eighty-six. But he don't talk. No, he don't say much at all."

Then I watched some sandlot baseball, at 9 PM, Yukon Standard Time. The newness of our marriage, when I started on this trip, makes it seem scarcely believable as a fact. Rather, it's a relief to remember that I have a powerful tie to go back to, and the memory of a relationship that was so good—and that was saving me, that gave my life meaning, with the coming child, and that made the future possible—that had brought the previous barrenness to a close. I remember, too, how John Muir, in 1880, came back early from Alaska for the birth of Wanda, his first baby.

JULY 18

Hans Anderson was sleeping today at noon, when I went by, just as he usually was in 1966—his sleeping feet sticking off the end of the couch. At the garage, they're busy cleaning a big cross-continental truck with a steam hose. The girder trailers are gone, but others are parked in their place, while the drivers sleep. The taxi drivers wear jokers' hats and kid each other like jack-in-the-box kids. And here and there, sits the traditional jumpy, muddy millionaire of this region, with a face like a bull's, who found gold or some other mineral, or has fucked the Indians over good.

JULY 19

I woke up this morning to the creaking of seagulls. Everywhere there are seagulls. Also helicopters, so that one wonders at the existence of the former, as the latter proliferate. The Oldest Trapper came out of Hans Anderson's second shack, in the clump of cabins, to go to the outhouse. "Private Outhouse," it says. I was reading Updike in another outhouse, which had partly tipped over. It's a central occasion for an old man and he had put his hat on, and felt his way slowly, staying inside thereafter for a long while.

I'm having considerable trouble seeing Skook. Each morning, over the radio, he keeps denying me permission to fly in. As well as my young man's luck of the trip in 1966, my young man's joy is gone also. And meanwhile, alone, I fantasize the mad stuff—being spun, blindfolded and nude, at a ladies' party, with a stud's hard-on. Today, for the third day, the Indian girl who cooks for Skook didn't show up from her visit home to her relatives in Fort St. John, and his venturesome, hoarse old voice on the radio said that although it would be "fine and dandy" for me to come when she returned: not before. So, I'm still stranded in this driftwood town—rather like a seaport for its impermanence and its strange personalities.

The dogs in the cars are bigger than the people. They stand in the back seat and lean half over the front. Aimlessly energetic, dark Indians live on the Liard River, at a hamlet called Two-and-a-half Mile, and taxi in, and later home again. There's a guy with drastic, deep, overlapped scars across his forehead, who got drunk and went head-first through his windshield. Another guy has painted his cabin with half-moons and stars. An Indian woman goes by, carrying her arm wrapped in a sling of tied gauze, and with a man's jacket over her shoulders, a pink shawl tied round her head, and wearing a man's shoes. Her companion has on a black cowboy hat. A red-faced white man in a panel truck (everybody, of course, has a vehicle, if only in order to work on it), with a long- and fluffy-haired Indian girlfriend, has all of her brothers and sisters also in the truck. Her mother is in the hospital with TB for the coming several months. As soon as they got hitched up, he says, her mother went into the hospital, and all of the kids moved in with him. He's trying to hire a plane to fly to a claim on the Ross River for less than 130 dollars, he says.

A pair of jade-hunters from Edmonton have a jade-green airplane. And everyone in this vast space speaks of "staying in" (for the winter), or of "going out." The town is comprised of misshapen, cheapjack shacks and dustied-silver, half-crippled trailers; and there are the transient girls waiting-on-table, and the four bearded bulldozer operators making out with them. The real weirdos, however, are the highway folk—the helmeted, silent motorcyclists who stop for a minute to rest their kidneys—people engrossed in their bizarre long-distance feats and hang-ups. Strange, lonely, beetle-faced, obsessive types (at least I'm not acting mine out). At each garage are great, destroyed heaps of tires. The truckers periodically go round their wheels thumping with a hammer on the rubber to hear the timbre of the sound.

As for Skook, here are some informational bits from his pilot, Stan Bridenti. He has about eighty horses hanging close to camp and maybe twenty more that drift wild up the Kechika River, towards the Frog and Gataga forks. Last winter he flew in eight tons of oats to get them through a bad spell. Throughout the winter it's so windy, however, the wind bares the sidehills, and, except for drifts, even the valley floor carries only eighteen inches of permanent snow. Because Skook's teeth are all out now, he eats no meat and doesn't need to hunt. Eats lots of eggs, instead, and bread and rice, and keeps a couple of Indian boys there through the winter to bring in wood, feed the horses, and for company, of course. Talks every day on the radio at eleven o'clock. His hips are so crippled, he walks like he has a bean up his ass, but he's so strong in the shoulders he can still throw a one-hundred-pound pack box onto a horse, though he doesn't ride. Even when he did, and hunted, he wouldn't allow the mountain sheep to be shot that the snows force down into his valley.

My trip, by and large, has been a failure, I think, and I've learned I no longer like to hitchhike—to subjugate myself to someone else, have to accept tacitly whatever they say, or let their scheduling be the law of the land. I've learned that my boyish luck and glee have worn out, and unhindered satisfaction from life may be more difficult to obtain from now on. But insofar as I came back to replace the material for a future novel that I used up in *Notes from the Century Before*, I may have succeeded rather than failed; and I also came back to "revisit the scene of the crime" of that book, since I might well never come back again.

Went to a Friday-night fest in the Watson Lake Hotel, with an old-time, white-whiskered fiddler and an old-man guitarist, and bear skins plastered on the wall—fatties and floozies reeling, rye-and-water and hot rum standing in pitchers on the bar, along with a basket of greenhouse lilacs. (Since there is no soil here, some of the women have pocket greenhouses.) An adding machine stands on top of the cash drawer for recording the take. Half of the patrons fell asleep in their chairs, but the others were shambling with appealing clumsiness on the dance floor—fat, fat white ladies with prominent diamond rings, but who, sadly, were not in fact married. Bars must legally close at 12:30, oddly enough. There was some pinching and stroking done by the men, who looked rather like husky boys blown up super-sized with a bicycle pump, and outside, as we walked away, we could hear giggling and bedding-down going on in the cabs of some of the pickups and freight trucks parked for the night. By 3 AM the sky gets fully light again. One guy nudged me and rolled his eyes in comradely, complimentary fashion when I told him I had been married twice. Except for their puffed-up size, many of the men are like the Upper West Side white men who live in Broadway hotels with the Negroes who are available to be picked up. My taxi man was in "highway transport," he said, and is "not ambitious. I don't want to be a millionaire, don't want to have women hanging off me, don't want a lot of divorces, don't want to have a heart attack." He wants a "cook" (a squaw) who'll live with him and darn his socks, and he can take off and fish or take his gun and go out hunting whenever he wants.

Skook's "girl" whose return I'm waiting for, incidentally, is named Mabel Frank. She's thirty-five or so; she's Indian; and she is said to be drunk in Fort St. John on her advance pay for the fall.

"Boy, that Skook could mount and breed," they say. They measure their manhood here by the number of squaws a man could screw, all free. And they've got one phrase that they use about mineral claims: "It'll make a mine." Skook would mix his bannock with grease right in the flour sack. Once he was starting off on a trip into the bush with a kid. "When do we pick up our groceries?" asks the kid. "Don't worry about grub. We'll pick 'em up when we get there!" Skook was packing an extra peg leg for the peg-leg trader at Fort Grahame to trade for supplies.

In Vancouver, wearing his red shirt and his big hat, he'd walk into a drug store looking for "castration clamps." Going into the bank, he yelled, "Don't worry. I'm not here to hold you up. Put this in the sugar bowl for me!" (Three or four hundred dollars.) On the street, he'd take off his hat to a lady. "I'm not picking you up. We've got better-looking squaws in the Yukon!" He's pretty badly "stove up" now, but in his time, "Nothing was too big for him." "Loon shit for supper!" he yelled once, when his float plane looked about to crash. Another time, bellying up to a bar for a drink, Skook saw a brawl starting. He kicked out the lights to go into it. He was with George Rifle. "Come help me, George. I've got somebody here I can't handle," he hollered. "Leggo, you damn fool, it's me you got," George hollered back. When he was drunk, they carried him out of the bar on a tarp, and when the hunting season started, he'd line up his Indian boys at the bar and treat them to a last drink, having bought each of them a new black hat and a vermilion shirt, and they "idolized him." Once he was so tired "he had to lean up against a tree to cough." His lead dog then was a black bear, and it could line out so fast it was a hundred yards away before the rest of the team first hit the ground. But a grizzly treed it, and the sled and dogs and Skook and all were hanging from the top limb, one time.

"Lousy Lou" was his more recent girlfriend—an Indian woman he used to come in and shag once in a while, having spent one thousand dollars at Christmas treating everybody to drinks. (That white woman he sent the rocking chair to, in the Cariboo country, never married, and finally died.) Skook is very tough, rumoured to have killed a guy once and put him under the ice of the Liard, with marks as if he had fallen off a bridge. At least, the Indians think someone may have murdered him. More likely, though, he pawned his own things to buy liquor, and nobody would admit afterward to having helped him do that. "Siwash," and "Johnny-boy," are whites' names for Indians. A day's walk out along the Dease River from Lower Post lives (or lived) an old coot who seems to have disappeared. The "Johnny-boys" turn their eyes up if you mention him, because he used to take shots at them. He tacked notes all over his door with old cartridge casings, saying that he'd hang the man who broke in—he even drew pictures of men hanging. Once the Mountie came to look around, and took home some of the pictures to show to his wife. The roof was all spruce bark, cut and laid flat. And he had a big wooden radio dating to 1936—he was sane back then, the storekeeper says. He had log dog-houses covered with moss, and trees ringed for firewood for a quarter of a mile around his cabin. Also moosehorns lying on the ground, each with the date when he'd shot the animal carved into it, like carving in soap. He had a bunch of meat-cutting boards which he'd carefully hewn with his axe and hoped to sell in town. Once a year the old bugger would come in and collect a whole year's worth of pension checks and buy an entire year's groceries, all at once—tough like Skook.

Around Christmastime, the old Indians who live alone in the bush are likely to get hold of a gallon of wine and pass out in their cabins and freeze to death quietly, as they lie there stretched out. And when you come to get them, he says, with a narrow dogsled, of course with rigor mortis, they don't fit, or their frozen arms catch in the under-growth, going out. So, old Skook (or him), they'd chop the

Indians' arms right off and put them beside him in the sled like neatly stacked sticks. The guy, at the end, might have shriveled up from TB to a rack of bones, "110 pounds soaking wet and wearing his chaps"—although he'd once won the annual flour-packing contest, down in Teslin.

As an outfitter, Skook had a fetish for white horses; would pay top dollar for them. I should mention that I didn't simply charter the Super Cub and fly out to Skook's place and force myself on him, because I felt sorry for him in his position—didn't want to impose on his kindness, which is as well-known as his Skookum toughness. There are these four types remaining from the old Lower Post prospecting crew. Hans Anderson—gentle, and sleeping in his clothes and boots fourteen hours a day. And Skook—still indomitable. And the white-bearded, nostalgic millionaire who made his pile on an asbestos mine and lives here on his fame, joking that he wants to organize the Indian girls so they'll stop "giving it away." And the stuffed, gross figure of an ex-cowboy whose father became a famous packer on the Telegraph Trail after fleeing North Dakota as a crook, but who himself appears merely papier mâché, and as a garage man works on casualties of the Alcan Highway.

The bar girls from other bars came into our Watson Lake Hotel, as the evening progressed. The whole population was sleepy with beer. The owner and "wife" had a fight, throwing the phone book at one another. She had to take over the bar. "I came into this world working hard and I guess I'll go out of it that way too," she said. Much talk about two barefoot English girls swimming in the raw in the Liard; and squaws getting bred. And a guy being given the blanket-toss in a bear skin that stunk to high heaven. And about a pilot with doughnut wheels on his Piper Cub who could land on a river's gravel bar by skipping his wheels off the water, as he came in.

Then, a rainy night for me, tearing down the Alcan Highway, past the usual grim assortment of traffic, with a French Canadian on the bus who claimed to have fought in the Congo with both Moise Tshombe *and* Che Guevara. Also a pale foreign boy who doesn't speak English; a dumbbell from the Adirondacks; and a self-described "animal." The curious, endless stick forest, with an occasional single cabin with the word STORE on it. British Columbia has put up signs for each river or creek, Coal River, Rabbit River, but the mud bespatters them almost illegibly. The road runs alongside or in sight of or at the foot of mountains most of the way. At 5 AM we were at Muncho Lake (Mile 463 of the Alcan Highway—Watson Lake is at 642), and just about even with Skook's Terminus Mountain, to the west. The road has no intimacy, but it's wild. "Jenny," as if from the Bronze Age, and going to Fort Nelson, materializes by the side of the road at Toad River—what errand has brought her out? There's a valley full of yellow gravel, with a small creek running in it. This is country thirty years raw—country driven on only for thirty years. And I do recommend the journey for gorging on, gulping down sheer zigzag geography.

On a bus, the boyish positions one stretches or crumples into. One guy is spending the whole trip to Dawson Creek coughing and hawking. Low mushy clouds all the way, making the hills and buttes seem like mountains. Fort Nelson is a scatter-spit town of 1,200 souls with oil wells. The ticket agent is reading *Anna Karenina*, the first good book I've seen in somebody's hands for the last six weeks. There's an Indian aboard in a saffron shirt, and a hulk of a man with flat, pancake ears, and a guy with a silent giggle—he says he went "Outside," and went to church, and saw them taking the collection with a bag on the end of a fishing pole. Speaks about "duck soup," and people "getting wise" to something. I always assume that strangers are friends with each other, even on the NYC subway. Just carry matches and fishing tackle, he says; you don't need a rifle or radio.

There was no soil in Watson Lake, and there's still no soil. In Alaska, of course, they have soil in some places and the vegetables grow big and fast, but taste hollow and watery. Lunch at Trutch (Mile 200), on thin soup, served with the knowledge that they'll never see us again. There's the lean, short, hardy squaw who moves with a motion like skating, and then the gypsy-matron type, the international, all-things-to-all-folk mother. It's very painful to leave the bush, even not considering that I've not accomplished what I had hoped, and even considering that I'm going home to Marion, and the birth of our baby in four months, and this numbing, thousand-mile bus trip is a help to ease me out.

The whole northern sky is full of a rainstorm and clouds that do everything *except* rain. Finally, spitting gusts. Just before Dawson Creek we get into poplared, homestead country with soil and green fields and a paved highway. The farmers among the tourists feel relieved and talk about "going to town." As at last we pulled into Edmonton, the psychosomatics of relief hit me with a sudden sore throat. I stayed overnight in a hotel which had an elevator, and a stoplight outside. So, down from the mountains to the great plains, with three realizations: that my trip was not as I had hoped it would be; that I've verged into middle age; and that the wilderness really is finished, done for, right now, and, in fact, is probably to be more satisfyingly explored in my own imagination than in reality.

The Canadians are a muted version of Americans, lacking our worst and also our best qualities. I sat, by a clerical error, in the first-class part of the plane east from Edmonton (after a day at their "Klondike Days"), and noticed how fat the seat belt seemed. It was so easy and quick getting from one place to another by now, but the mechanics and manoeuvres—gate to gate and desk to desk—seemed intolerably time-consuming, though in fact I was travelling four-thousand miles in the amount of time it had been taking me to go one hundred by truck. We had had tranquillizing music and then the roar of the jet in take-off, all of us pausing a moment, with the brief thread of our consciousness in the balance. We lived.

Later, we circled over Bridgeport, Connecticut, for an hour and a half because of a strike of air traffic controllers. My taxi driver got out of the cab at the toll plaza of the Battery Tunnel and into a fight with the driver behind him. Then I was home, finally—a mess on the floor, and nothing accomplished in the way of moving in—even a brief fight with Marion. Earrings on the floor, a kinky necklace rattling from the doorknob. But oh the delicious complexity! The fullness of life again—pregnancy, difficulty, and beauty.

Epilogue

My daughter, Molly, was born in fine fettle that November. She grew up in Greenwich Village, went off to Harvard, then acquired a master's degree in European history, and married an actor, with whom she lives in Brooklyn. They have two sons. My own marriage lasted for twenty-five years.

This journal, meanwhile, arising also from an early season in my professional life, remained in notebook form until the next century, when Lauren Seidman, a former student of mine—finding the handwriting still legible compared to my scribblings from Alaskan and African trips twenty or thirty years later—painstakingly transcribed it. The travelling in British Columbia during 1960, 1966, and 1968 that I was privileged to do retains the tender aura of a first love in my mind's eye (like

trouping with the Ringling Bros. Circus ten years earlier);
and except for one jaunt by train from Prince Rupert to
Montreal in 1986, I've never been back. Thus the mammoth environmental changes I've watched inflicted upon
other places I've loved are not known to me in a Canadian
context first-hand. Nevertheless, my pessimism for the
wider world, ecologically, economically, meteorologically,
oceanographically, is profound. Already having witnessed
famine, for example, in the Sudan, I'm glad to be seventy-
five, so as not to be obliged to witness any more.

Yet to live is to see, and for a young person, all eyes,
bristling with energy, there seems to have been no dimi-
nution of opportunities to explore new ground. Again and
again in this century, from Tibet to Lake Victoria, simple
frailty has prevented me from embarking on the kind of
journey of interviews in raw country I used to do. Sharing
now the infirmities that my best sources used to have, and
with countless old-timer memories of my own, I wish the
descendants of the individuals described here eternal good
fortune. I've left terminology such as "Indian" unchanged,
since this is a period piece.

Otherwise, what happened to me in 1968 was discov-
ering that I was primarily an essayist, not a novelist, as I
had dreamed. My previous books, published in 1956, 1960,
and 1965, had been fiction, set in the worlds of a three-
ring circus, of professional boxing, and of streetwise New
York—each the product of on-the-ground witnessing, such

as I had lately attempted in Manson Creek. In fact, my purpose here had been to gather impressions for what would become my fourth novel, situated on the Canadian frontier in the 1880s, *Seven Rivers West*. This book did appear a couple of decades later, after off-and-on effort, while in the meantime I began writing essays like a house afire. *Notes from the Century Before,* my earlier account of a trip to the adjoining region—the Stikine and Spatsizi rivers, the villages of Atlin and Telegraph Creek—was published in 1969, winning a readership that has kept it in print in paperback editions ever since. Yet even before that encouragement, my new marriage, to a woman who was herself a magazine editor, coupled with Molly's triumphant birth, as well as possibly the liberating effect of my minatory father's death a year or two earlier, seemed to free my tongue to address the reader informally in personal essays without needing to veil my observations as fiction.

For a lifelong stutterer this was a doubly jubilant transition. I could just speak to people, and by 1971 my first collection, *The Courage of Turtles,* came out. Then in two years, another, and in three more, a third: which, together, were soon sieved to select a reader. During the 1970s, although I spent two spells with Cajun trappers in the swamps of southwest Louisiana learning how they lived off the land, most of my travels were in Africa. *African Calliope* was the result. And whereas for my circus novel I'd cared for lions in their cages (sometimes sleeping under the cages when we played the same town under canvas two nights in a row), in Kenya and Tanzania I slept on their own level on the veldt, revelling in their grunts and roars. I revelled, too, in the huge audience an essay could attain in a national magazine, not forgetting to remind myself that Montagne's *Essais* predated even *Don Quixote* by a quarter century.

Nonetheless, as a youngster I'd yearned to be a novelist, not an essayist, and so the chimera of *Seven Rivers West* kept recurring as an unconsummated ambition. My central character was going to try to pursue, then capture Bigfoot to display as a sideshow attraction back East. During the 1980s, with my boyhood fascination for Africa temporarily allayed, I rambled repeatedly by boat or float plane along the Yukon and Kuskokwim rivers in Alaska— or the Porcupine, the Colville, the Susitna, the Copper— interviewing prospectors, talking wildlife, scanning trails, sleeping among the sled dogs in a village like Fort Yukon, or by the Chukchi or the Bering seas. I read Pierre Burton and Raymond Patterson; ate moose, caribou, squirrel, muskrat, bobcat, and black bear meat; logged hours ogling wolf packs and grizzlies; met Athapaskans who had encountered Bigfoot in the bush—had chased one of them all summer in the Brooks Range trying to retrieve a kidnapped sister, perhaps, or had fed a silent, starving, hairy family that simply materialized at a trapline camp on a winter evening. Those seven rivers required individual invention, a tailored wealth of detail. But I had seen the Peace and the Parsnip, the Skeena and the North Thompson, so that novel came out successfully in 1986. As the cliché says, try what you dream.

I returned to essay-writing, taught at an accumulating total of ten colleges in a forty-year career with a good deal of pleasure, and travelled to Africa twice more during the 1990s, and to India twice also, plus Antarctica and Yemen; later, China and Uganda yet again. For a decade I wrote *New York Times* nature editorials and edited a thirty-volume nature-classics series for Penguin Books. So if this journal doesn't end cheerfully enough, it should have. I rode around New York Harbor on tugboats as well as down the Yukon. The next forty years were going to be quite splendid.

. . . .

Edward Hoagland